Culture and
Customs of
Chile

Culture and Customs of Chile

∽◦∾

Guillermo I. Castillo-Feliú

Culture and Customs of Latin America
and the Caribbean
Peter Standish, Series Editor

GREENWOOD PRESS
Westport, Connecticut • London

Library of Congress Cataloging-in-Publication Data

Castillo-Feliú, Guillermo I.
    Culture and customs of Chile / Guillermo I. Castillo-Feliú.
        p. cm.—(Culture and customs of Latin America and the Caribbean, ISSN 1521–8856)
    Includes bibliographical references (p. -) and index.
    ISBN 0–313–30783–0 (alk. paper)
    1. Chile—Civilization—20th century.   2. Chile—Social life and customs—20th century.   3. Arts, Modern—20th century—Chile.   4. Arts, Chilean.   5. Popular culture—Chile.   I. Title.   II. Series.
F3099.C286   2000
983.06'4—dc21   99–058879

British Library Cataloguing in Publication Data is available.

Library of Congress Catalog Card Number: 99–058879
ISBN: 0–313–30783–0
ISSN: 1521–8856

First published in 2000

Greenwood Press, 88 Post Road West, Westport, CT 06881
An imprint of Greenwood Publishing Group, Inc.
www.greenwood.com

Printed in the United States of America

The paper used in this book complies with the
Permanent Paper Standard issued by the National
Information Standards Organization (Z39.48–1984).

10 9 8 7 6 5 4 3 2 1

All photographs have been provided by the author. Map by Magellan Geographix.

Puro Chile es tu cielo azulado
(Pure Chile, blue is your sky)

> —Eusebio Lillo, September 17, 1847

Contents

Illustrations

Series Foreword

"CULTURE" is a problematic word. In everyday language we tend to use it in at least two senses. On the one hand we speak of cultured people and places full of culture, uses that imply a knowledge or presence of certain forms of behavior or of artistic expression that are socially prestigious. In this sense large cities and prosperous people tend to be seen as the most cultured. On the other hand, there is an interpretation of "culture" that is broader and more anthropological; culture in this broader sense refers to whatever traditions, beliefs, customs, and creative activities characterize a given community—in short, it refers to what makes that community different from others. In this second sense, everyone has culture; indeed, it is impossible to be without culture.

The problems associated with the idea of culture have been exacerbated in recent years by two trends: less respectful use of language and a greater blurring of cultural differences. Nowadays, "culture" often means little more than behavior, attitude, or atmosphere. We hear about the culture of the boardroom, of the football team, of the marketplace; there are books with titles like *The Culture of War* by Richard Gabriel (Greenwood, 1990) or *The Culture of Narcissism* by Christopher Lasch (1979). In fact, as Christopher Clausen points out in a recent article published in the *American Scholar* (Summer 1996), we have gotten ourselves into trouble by using the term so sloppily.

People who study culture generally assume that culture (in the anthropological sense) is learned, not genetically determined. Another general assumption made in these days of multiculturalism has been that cultural differences should be respected rather than put under pressure to change. But these assumptions, too, have sometimes proved to be problematic. For instance, multiculturalism is a fine ideal, but in practice it is not always easy to reconcile with the beliefs of the very people who advocate it: for example, is female circumcision an issue of human rights or just a different cultural practice?

The blurring of cultural differences is a process that began with the steamship, increased with radio, and is now racing ahead with the Internet. We are becoming globally homogenized. Since the English-speaking world (and the United States in particular) is the dominant force behind this process of homogenization, it behooves us to make efforts to understand the sensibilities of members of other cultures.

This series of books, a contribution toward that greater understanding, deals with the neighbors of the United States, with people who have just as much right to call themselves Americans. What are the historical, institutional, religious, and artistic features that make up the modern culture of such peoples as the Haitians, the Chileans, the Jamaicans, and the Guatemalans? How are their habits and assumptions different from our own? What can we learn from them? As we familiarize ourselves with the ways of other countries, we come to see our own from a new perspective.

Each volume in the series focuses on a single country. With slight variations to accommodate national differences, each begins by outlining the historical, political, ethnic, geographical, and linguistic context, as well as the religious and social customs, and then proceeds to a discussion of a variety of artistic activities, including the press, the media, the cinema, music literature, and the visual and performing arts. The authors are all intimately acquainted with the countries concerned: some were born or brought up in them, and each has a professional commitment to enhancing the understanding of the culture in question.

We are inclined to suppose that our ways of thinking and behaving are normal. And so they are . . . for us. We all need to realize that ours is only one culture among many, and that it is hard to establish by any rational criteria that ours as a whole is any better (or worse) than any other. As individual members of our immediate community, we know that we must learn to respect our differences from one another. Respect for differences between cultures is no less vital. This is particularly true of the United States, a nation of immigrants, but one that sometimes seems to be bent on destroying variety at home, and, worse still, on having others follow suit. By learning about other people's cultures, we come to understand and respect them; we earn their respect for us; and, not least, we see ourselves in a new light.

Peter Standish
East Carolina University

Introduction

WHEN SPANISH CONQUISTADORS first arrived in the New World at the end of the fifteenth century, Chile was an unknown quantity, for it was not until the fourth decade of the next century that explorers began to venture south of what is today Central America. Francisco Pizarro conquered the Inca empire with lightning speed in 1533 when he had Atahualpa, the last Inca emperor, executed and gold-rich Peru fell into Spanish hands. Chile was at that time simply a far-off land, known for its fierce inhabitants and little else. When Pedro de Valdivia arrived in the Central Valley in 1541, he was disappointed to find little gold and an enemy who was as implacable as he himself was.

Chile developed far removed from most of the rest of Latin America, isolated by geography and by its great distance from the better known and more accessible centers of the Spanish empire. The relative lack of gold and silver, especially compared with those which conquistador Hernán Cortés had found in Mexico and Pizarro had found in Peru, allowed this southernmost Spanish colony to develop in relative peace and stability.

After Chile attained its independence from Spain during the second decade of the nineteenth century, the new nation's government promoted immigration from Europe. The new settlers established strong roots in the land, promoted the creation of stable governments, and helped the new nation achieve a relatively homogeneous population and a growing middle class. In this last respect, Chile paralleled its trans-Andean neighbors, Argentina and Uruguay, as well as the Central American nation of Costa Rica.

This unique combination of factors—geography, isolation, and political

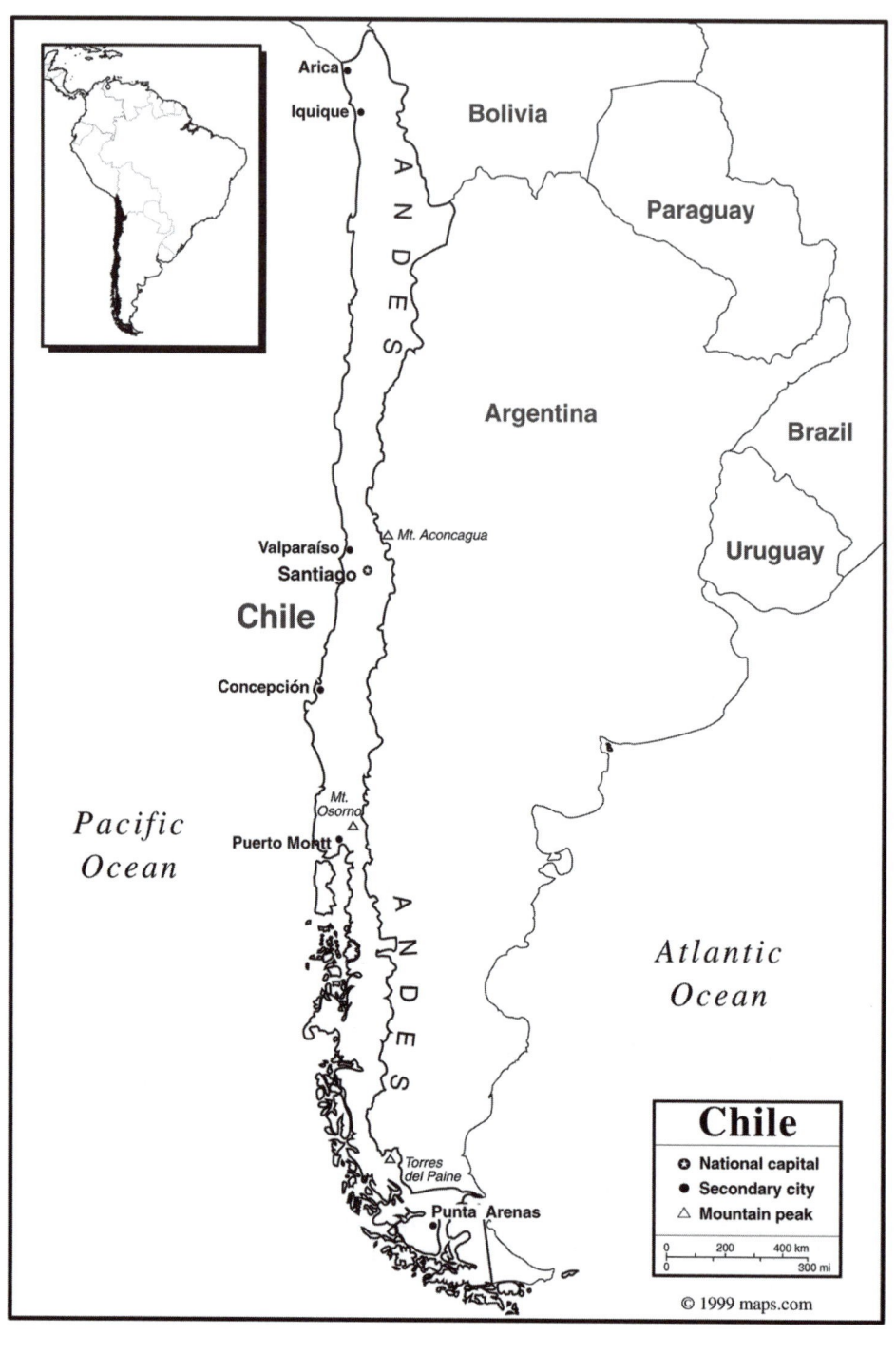

Arica

Iquique

Bolivia

Paraguay

Argentina

Brazil

△ *Mt. Aconcagua*

Valparaíso

Santiago

Uruguay

Chile

Concepción

*Pacific
Ocean*

Mt.
Osorno
△
Puerto Montt

*Atlantic
Ocean*

A N D E S

△ *Torres
del Paine*

Punta Arenas

Chile

- ⊙ **National capital**
- ● **Secondary city**
- △ **Mountain peak**

0	200	400 km
0		300 mi

© 1999 maps.com

stability and continuity—helped Chile to be less in the news than other Latin American nations, such as Mexico, Cuba, Brazil, and the smaller countries of Central America. Not very long ago, many average Americans had never heard of Chile or, if they had, had only a vague notion of its location, its economic significance, or its political history. The events that began shortly before 1970 placed this nation in the forefront of the world's consciousness.

The coming to power of the world's first freely elected Marxist, the Socialist Salvador Allende, in September 1970 placed Chile squarely on the political map. The world rapidly became aware of the existence of this long, thin country, and the three-year political experiment kept it in the headlines for much of the thirty-some months of the Allende presidency. The coup d'état that toppled the Marxist government in 1973, the accession to power of General Augusto Pinochet, and the sixteen years of military dictatorship that ensued, ensured Chile's remaining in the world's consciousness.

By the time democracy returned to Chile at the end of 1989, the country's economy had undergone a significant change. The Chilean peso had stabilized, exports of Chile's wines and fruit had skyrocketed, and many, if not all, of the attendant economic problems had either disappeared or been attenuated. The middle class continued to grow, the poverty rate steadily dropped from a high of some 40 percent in 1970 to around 27 percent, and unemployment, which had been extremely high during the first years after the coup, had come down to the single digits by the mid-1990s. Suddenly, everyone seemed to know of Chile's existence, but the country's political, economic, and social stability effectively removed it from the world's headlines.

In October 1998, Augusto Pinochet, recently retired as commander in chief of the nation's armed forces and senator for life, traveled to London to undergo surgery at a private clinic. On October 16, shortly after his successful operation, Pinochet was placed under house arrest in London as a result of a petition by a Spanish judge, Baltazar Garzon, that Great Britain agree to extradite the former politician to stand trial in Spain for crimes allegedly committed by him against Spanish citizens during his tenure as Chile's president. Suddenly, Chile was again under scrutiny as its government, as well as British and Spanish courts and governments, sought to resolve the predicament. But the situation involving Chile, Great Britain, and Spain has implications that go far beyond the possible outcome of the Pinochet matter. Suddenly other world leaders, past and present, from First World as well as developing countries, are faced with the possibility that they might be held accountable for actions, real and perceived, and that such actions might be taken before national courts beyond their own nation's borders.

On March 2, 2000, after almost seventeen months under house arrest, Pinochet was released by order of British Minister Jack Straw, who found that medical exams conducted under his auspices determined that the general would be mentally and physically unable to withstand the rigors of a trial in Spain or in any of the other European countries which, during his stay in London, had requested his extradition. Back in Chile, a struggle has ensued between detractors and supporters of Pinochet as to whether or not he will be brought to trial for the alleged atrocities committed during his dictatorship.

But Chile is much more than the political events that have brought it to the world's attention. The present volume demonstrates that it is a nation possessing great natural beauty, a fascinating history, great cultural traditions, and a people known for their warm and welcoming nature. Although it has a relatively small population, especially compared with Mexico and Brazil, Chile has contributed greatly to the hemisphere's literature, education, and social maturity. Its political stability has been a model for most of the hemisphere's nations, and it stands today as an example of a nation that is successfully meeting its social responsibilities. In spite of its relatively recent turbulent past, Chile looks forward to political, social, and economic stability with a population that will be increasingly able to enjoy the fruits of its many achievements.

Chronology

1520	Portuguese navigator Ferdinand Magellan, sailing under the Spanish flag, finds a way through the treacherous waters north of Cape Horn, at the southern tip of South America. He sails northward through imposing and desolate fjords, protected from the rough waters of the Atlantic and Pacific Oceans, inside territory that later will form part of Chile. The strait that he discovers will later bear his name.
1536	Conquistador Diego de Almagro leads an expedition that travels south from Cuzco, Peru, and reaches Chile's Central Valley. Finding no gold, he returns to Peru.
1541	Don Pedro de Valdivia arrives in the Central Valley and, on February 12, founds Santiago atop Huelén Hill, which he renames Santa Lucía. Valdivia is later named governor of the Kingdom of Chile, a part of the Viceroyalty of New Castile (Peru).
1557–1810	Chile is governed by governors and captains general (the first of whom is García Hurtado de Mendoza) answerable to the viceroy of Peru, in Lima. In 1776, Charles III of Spain creates the Viceroyalty of Río de La Plata, which includes much of present-day Argentina, Uruguay, and Paraguay. Chile thus becomes the southernmost part of the Viceroyalty of New Castile. Subsequent conquests extend

Chile's reaches south to Chiloé, the largest of the nation's islands. In 1778, Charles III allows free trade between Chile and Spain, creating a new and growing merchant class that will prove crucial to the move for independence early in the nineteenth century.

1810	Spain, immersed in its own war of independence (against the troops of Napoleon Bonaparte, which have occupied the Iberian Peninsula since 1808), is too weak to stop the burgeoning move for separation. Chile declares its independence on September 18, 1810.
1814	With Napoleon defeated, Spain regains its independence and, renewed, begins the reconquest of Chile, an effort that will last until 1818.
1817	Argentine General José de San Martín crosses the Andes from Argentina and joins Chileans under the command of Bernardo O'Higgins in an effort to definitively defeat the Royalists. The two generals are ultimately successful, and Chile gains its independence the following year. O'Higgins becomes the new nation's first president. Chile's first constitution is promulgated in 1822 and lasts for eleven years.
1823	Slavery is abolished in Chile. A period of civil strife begins, and lasts until 1830, when the strong hand of General Minister Diego Portales puts an end to it. A long period of prosperity, constitutional government, and political tranquillity ensues.
1833	Diego Portales succeeds in promulgating a new constitution, based on an authoritative, presidential government. It lasts until 1891.
1836–1839	Chile fights a brief war against the Peruvian-Bolivian Confederation, afraid that this merger threatens its security and stability. It is successful, and the two nations once again are separated.
1866	Chile joins Peru in a war against Spain, begun when Spain bombs Chile's main port of Valparaíso and attempts to exert control over the country. The skirmish is short-lived, and Spain retires from the contest.

1879–1884   The War of the Pacific erupts between Chile and its former antagonists, Peru and Bolivia. It is occasioned by a long dispute over control of the nitrate fields which, although mostly inside Peruvian and Bolivian territory, have been managed mostly by Chilean interests. Chile's victory in 1884 effectively increases its national territory by one-third, shutting Bolivia off from direct access to the Pacific and leaving it landlocked. Chile's natural wealth increases substantially, and the economic benefit lasts until the outbreak of World War I in 1914.

1891   Civil war erupts in Chile, pitting the executive branch, under President José Manuel Balmaceda, against the Congress. The brief but bloody conflict is won by the legislative branch when its military backers succeed in overwhelming the support for Balmaceda. Balmaceda commits suicide.

1891–1925   A new constitution in 1891 establishes a parliamentary form of government; chief executives continue to serve five-year terms (a pattern established in 1871), until 1925, when the parliamentary system is abolished.

1920–1924   President Arturo Alessandri serves as chief executive, but his term of office is interrupted by political disagreements before its expiration.

1925   A new constitution is promulgated that reestablishes a republican form of government with a president as head of the executive branch. The chief executive is to be elected by the direct vote of the people for a term of six years. There can be no immediate reelection; the outgoing president is eligible to run again only after the passage of six years. There is a bicameral Congress, made up of a Senate and a Chamber of Deputies, its members also to be elected by the people. Suffrage is universal for those men eighteen and over. A judicial branch is also created, the Supreme Court, with its seat in Santiago.

1924–1932   A series of presidents are appointed, a brief military dictatorship ensues, and the nation lives through an eight-year period of strife in sharp contrast to more than a century of independence since 1818.

1932	Arturo Alessandri is reelected to serve a six-year term as president. A new period of political stability ensues that lasts until 1973.
1949	Women obtain the right to vote. Their influence and independence as voters become crucial in the political contests, significantly in the presidential elections of 1964.
1964–1970	Eduardo Frei Montalva is elected president of Chile, obtaining the first absolute majority of the vote (55.5 percent) in Chilean history, in a field of three candidates. Second place goes to Salvador Allende (39.5 percent), candidate of the Socialist party. It is Allende's third run for the presidency (the first was in 1952). Frei belongs to the Christian Democratic party, a centrist bloc that also exists in Europe. His term ends in 1970.
1970–1973	The presidential election has three major candidates: Jorge Alessandri, a former president (1958–1964), of the Partido Nacional (National party), a conservative group; Radomiro Tomic, of the Christian Democratic party; and, for the fourth time, Salvador Allende, supported by a coalition of leftist parties known as the Unidad Popular (Popular Unity), including the Socialists, Communists, and the Movimiento de Izquierda Revolucionaria (MIR, Movement of the Revolutionary Left). Tomic obtains 27.8 percent of the vote; Allende, 36.3 percent; and Alessandri, 34.9 percent. Allende is approved by the Congress as Chile's president for the term 1970–1976.
1973	Following three years of political and social strife, as well as economic disruption, Salvador Allende is toppled by Chile's armed forces during the early morning hours of September 11. President Allende apparently commits suicide inside the Moneda, the presidential palace, and a military junta takes over the government. The coup d'état, referred to as the Pronunciamiento (Pronouncement) by military chiefs, is headed by Gen. Augusto Pinochet who later is named president.

1973–1989   The armed forces, with Pinochet as their leader, puts Congress in recess. For the next sixteen years, Chile ceases to be a democracy and is ruled by dictatorship. A new constitution, promulgated in 1981, institutionalizes what is referred to as a protected democracy. In 1988, a "Sí o No" referendum is called for, and Chileans are able to vote freely on their country's political future. A "Yes" vote would mean that Pinochet would remain as president until 1998; a "No" vote would mean that new, open elections would be held in late 1989; Pinochet could choose to run in such an election if he so desired.

1988   The "Yes or No" vote is carried out freely and openly. The "Sí" voters, those who want Pinochet to remain in power, cast 44 percent of the vote. The "No" voters win with a majority of 56 percent. Pinochet agrees to step down at the end of 1989, after the open elections. Political parties reform and preparations begin to return to the electoral process.

1989–1993   In December, a Christian Democrat, Patricio Aylwin, is elected to a single four-year term; Chile returns to its democratic tradition although there are still links to the past dictatorship as Augusto Pinochet remains as commander in chief of the armed forces until his final retirement in March 1998. Shortly after his departure from the military, Pinochet is named senator for life, according to a provision placed in the 1981 constitution.

1993–1999   Aylwin is succeeded by a Christian Democrat, Eduardo Frei Ruiz-Tagle, son of Eduardo Frei Montalva, president from 1964 to 1970. He obtains an absolute majority of the popular vote, slightly higher than his father had obtained in 1964. His term of office runs until December 1999, when new elections take place.

1998   Augusto Pinochet travels to London to undergo surgery. The operation is successful, and he plans to remain in London to recover. While there, a Spanish judge, Baltazar Garzón, asks the government of Great Britain to allow extradition of Pinochet to Spain, to be tried there by a Spanish court for crimes allegedly committed against Spanish citizens in Chile during the military dictatorship.

1999 Elections for the presidency held on December 12 for the six-year term 2000–2006. Ricardo Lagos, Socialist party and candidate of the Concertación, supported by the outgoing government, and Joaquín Lavín, Conservative, split most of the votes, each receiving some 47 percent. The other candidates split the remaining four to five percent. A runoff election, the first in Chile's history, is scheduled for January 16, between Lagos and Lavín.

2000 On January 16, Ricardo Lagos obtains 51.31 percent of the vote to Joaquín Lavín's 48.69 percent and becomes president-elect for the term beginning March 11.

General Augusto Pinochet is freed from house arrest in London, on Thursday, March 2, by order of British Minister Jack Straw. Straw decides that the medical exams carried out by British medical personnel point to the general's being physically and mentally unable to withstand the rigors of a trial. A Chilean air force plane takes Pinochet back to Chile, where the general faces a still uncertain legal future.

2000 On March 2, British minister Jack Straw releases Augusto Pinochet, finding that medical exams conducted in London had determined that the general would be mentally and physically unable to withstand the rigors of a trial in Spain. The general returns to Chile.

1

Context

Chile, fertile and distinguished province
Famous in the Antarctic region,
Respected in distant lands
As strong, illustrious and powerful,
Has produced a race so upstanding,
So proud, gallant and bellicose,
That never by kings has it been conquered,
Nor by foreigners subjugated.
    (Alonso de Ercilla y Zúñiga, *The Araucaniad* [translation by
    G. I. Castillo-Feliú])

CHILE'S UNIQUENESS

WHEN SPANISH POET/SOLDIER Alonso de Ercilla y Zúñiga wrote these words
in the continent's first epic poem, *La Araucana*, published in three parts
between 1569 and 1589, he perhaps unknowingly placed Chile on the map
in geographical, historical, ethnic, and literary terms, for it is indisputably
this work of literature which Chileans today perceive to be the seminal foundation of their national identity. Ercilla lauds the military prowess, the character, and the bravery of the Spanish conquistadors and of the Araucanians,
also known as Mapuches (People of the Land), the native inhabitants of
central Chile who struggled against one another for control of that area.
Steeped in the classics, Ercilla's poetic brush creates heroes reminiscent of
those painted by Homer in the *Iliad*, among them Colo Colo, Lautaro,

Galvarino, and Caupolicán, elected democratically to lead the Araucanians against the invading Europeans.

When the conquistador Diego de Almagro arrived in Chile, various groups of natives received the common name of Mapuches. They sometimes were at war against each other, and at other times united for the common defense against common enemies.

The Picunches (People of the North) lived between the Choapa and the Itata rivers, an area some 285 kilometers (175 miles) north of Santiago. The Moluches (Warriors) inhabited the area between the Bío-Bío and Toltén rivers. One of Chile's most important and largest rivers, the Bío-Bío empties in the sea at Concepción. The Toltén River stretches between Lake Villarrica, one of Chile's most beautiful bodies of water, and the ocean at Toltén. The area in between these two rivers today includes Concepción and Temuco, the latter a growing center with the largest concentration of Mapuche culture. Some of the other native tribes are the Puelches (People of the East), who live near the Andes and east of Temuco, and the Fueguinos, a primitive group that lives in Tierra del Fuego. The latter tribe was subdivided into three groups: the Onas, hunters and fishermen; the Alacalufes (People Who Travel in Canoes), mostly fishermen; and the Yaganes, nomadic fishermen. Tierra del Fuego (Land of Fire) was given its name by the first Spaniards who sailed up the fjords of southern Chile and saw the fires built by the natives to keep warm in their cold and windy environment.

Most people nowadays use the terms Mapuche and Araucano synonymously, but the latter was applied by the first Spaniards only to those indigenous people they encountered between the Bío-Bío and Toltén rivers. It is this mainly this group, then, that Ercilla immortalized in his epic poem.

The name "Chili" is of fairly ancient origin. It had been used by the inhabitants of pre-Columbian Chile long before the arrival of the Europeans. There are at least two hypotheses as to its origin, and probably one has as much validity as the other one.

Some people think there might be a connection with the English word "chilly," although this is almost certainly simply a coincidence. In Quechua, the language spoken by the Incas, *Tchilli*, meaning "snow" or "cold," was the name given to the area around the Aconcagua River and its valley, north of Santiago and directly west of Mt. Aconcagua, across the border in Argentina. Natives referred to the region as *Chili-mapu* (Land of Chile), and the language that the people spoke was known as *Chili-dagu* (language of Chile).

The second hypothesis is that the people who first settled in the region chose the name in imitation of a native species of bird, today called the *trile*, which was very common 500 years ago. As these birds flew, they uttered the cry *chi-li, chi-li*. Peruvian Indians, who had fought the indigenous people to the south, carried back to Peru the name "Chili." The Spaniards, who soon traveled south to conquer and settle the new land, changed the final "i" to an "e" and thus, the present-day Chile.

Whichever hypothesis is closer to the truth—and perhaps neither is—the fact is that the country settled thousands of years ago, and conquered by the Spanish in the middle of the sixteenth century, is unique in many ways. The individuality of its citizens is certainly due to the many factors that join together to form the fascinating land that today is known as Chile.

The twentieth-century Chilean writer Benjamín Subercaseaux wrote the aptly titled *Chile o una loca geografía* (Chile or a Crazy Geography), published in 1940. Even a cursory examination of the country's appearance demonstrates what Subercaseaux implied in the very title of his work. The nation stretches some 2,700 miles from north to south, beginning at approximately the 17th parallel of south latitude, and ending precipitously at the 56th, a scant three to four degrees north of the continent of Antarctica. Countless means have been employed to add credence to the idea of the country's geographical uniqueness, ranging from the comparative to the almost ludicrous: Chile would fit almost exactly between New York City and Los Angeles or, equally, it would cover a strip extending from northern Scandinavia to beyond the boot tip of Italy; it is the longest country in the world measured from north to south; it is the country with the greatest variation in annual rainfall, ranging from absolutely none, in part of the northern Atacama Desert, where no precipitation has been measured in 400 years, to around 200 inches of rain that falls in the southern temperate forests. Chile is said to be so narrow that those wishing to clap and, at the same time, stay within the nation's political borders can do so only by facing either the Pacific or the Andes as they beat their hands together. The country is indeed rather slender: at its narrowest it is only some 90 miles wide, in the area of the archipelago south of the city of Puerto Montt; at its widest, it can reach some 250 miles, in the Atacama Desert. With a continental area of 286,396 square miles, Chile is larger than every European nation except Russia—larger than France or Spain, and almost three times the area of the United Kingdom. Texas, the state with the most comparable area, is, at 267,277 square miles, some 7 percent smaller than Chile.

Chile's climate and terrain are quite varied, as might be expected from the fact that the country stretches across some thirty-eight parallels, roughly equivalent to the distance from the northern tip of Africa to the northernmost part of Norway.

The Andes Mountains run the entire length of the country and significantly affect its climate, especially from the northern border to just south of Santiago, the capital. The Atacama Desert, which begins to disappear only just north of Santiago, owes its extreme dryness to these high mountains, which create a natural barrier for the rain-producing moisture that would normally come from the east.

Some of the highest peaks in the world are found from central Chile northward to its border with Peru and Bolivia, and along the Chilean-Argentine border as well. Ojos del Salado reaches an altitude of 6,880 meters (22,573 feet); Aconcagua, in Argentina but abutting Chile, is 6,959 meters high (22,832 feet); it is the highest peak in the New World, some 770 meters (2,500 feet) higher than Alaska's Mt. McKinley. Several other mountains range from 19,000 to 20,000 feet in altitude.

Santiago is only some 1,500 feet above sea level, much lower than other Latin American capitals such as Mexico City, Guatemala City, Bogotá, Quito, and La Paz. Yet, when the city's citizens glance in any direction, especially toward the east, they are struck by the majestic peaks of spectacular heights that once sealed off access to Argentina, especially during the winter. The highest peaks—Aconcagua is relatively close to Santiago—are always snowcapped; in summer the highest ones wear distinctive mantles atop their crests. In winter, between June and early August, when rains bathe the capital city, sometimes almost endlessly, these mantles grow downward until they almost become overcoats, even reaching the outskirts of the city. They deposit a light covering of snow and delight children even as they create minor havoc with the city's public utilities. Still, such occurrences are rare and many *santiaguinos* (Santiago residents) have to delve far back into their memories to recall the infrequent snowfalls that have been registered in the capital.

In 1972, a plane carrying Uruguayan rugby players attempted to fly across the Andes to Chile. The weather was poor, and the flight should have been postponed. The aircraft, a vintage, propeller-driven plane, crashed at an altitude of some 10,000 feet. Some of those aboard died, others, including some medical students, managed to survive and, after ten weeks of struggling against impossible odds and freezing temperatures, were rescued by a Chilean farmworker. The account of their harrowing experience was later made into a book and a film titled *Alive!*

In the early days of flight, planes, unable to fly above the mountains, had to navigate between peaks, when the weather allowed. Since the 1960s, jet planes have been able to fly 10,000 feet above the highest peaks, in summer or winter, permitting passengers to admire those forbidding mountaintops that once were impassable walls to travelers.

On the western side of the nation, the cold Humboldt current that starts in the southern Pacific skirts almost the entire length of the nation, markedly reducing the temperature of the waters that bathe the beautiful beaches of central Chile and, at the same time, appreciably cooling the air of the northernmost twenty or so parallels to below what might be expected at these latitudes. Thus, although the popular beaches that extend a few miles on either side of Valparaíso, at approximately 33 degrees south latitude, are crowded with sunbathers, in the warm months of summer, from mid-December through March, the relatively cool waters that lap the beaches (around 59° F) keep all but the hardiest from venturing into their frigid embrace for very long. This is quite a contrast with North America, where the Atlantic, which skirts the eastern seaboard at around the equivalent northern latitude—say near Hilton Head, South Carolina—has water temperatures that reach 87° F in August.

Shortly before the Humboldt Current nears Chile's northernmost city of Arica, on the border with Peru, the cold waters turn counterclockwise and continue skirting most of the coastal areas of Peru, creating a climate similar to that of the northern half of Chile. With this turn of events—or current, one might say—the waters off Arica reach an almost balmy 65°!

Temperatures from the 33rd parallel, approximately where Santiago is located, to the 56th parallel, where Chile ends, grow cooler. Summers are relatively mild, and often quite windy in the southernmost areas, with less moisture than during the winter, when precipitation is almost constant (mostly in the form of cold rain but also, sometimes, of snow). The average winter lows can reach 20° F, with lower temperatures at the higher elevations. Among the fjords of the archipelago are glaciers containing ice that is thousands of years old. Chile also lays claim to an area in Antarctica that is approximately 473,500 square miles in area, considerably larger than American Chile.

Since about 1990, Chileans and others have been able to visit the southern third of the country, beginning at Puerto Montt and usually ending at the city of Punta Arenas. In comfort, travelers can enjoy what Magellan and other explorers saw in the early sixteenth century as they ventured around the tip of the continent in search of a safer route that would take them toward completion of their circumnavigation of the Earth. The magnificence of the panorama afforded by a modern ship, which takes from three to six days to make the journey, is considered one of the highlights of the voyage.

The sheer variety of a country that stretches some 3,000 miles from north to south, covering almost an eighth of the planet's circumference, is striking. The area of the typical voyage's beginning, in Puerto Montt, is as green as might be expected for a region where rain is copious and temperatures are mild to cold. As the traveler moves south, nature becomes less hospitable but awesome. In the summer, from December through March, days are normally longer than in the Central Valley. This is the best time to travel here; the rest of the year can be extremely cold, rainy, or snowy, with harsh winds buffeting the ships.

The trip features glaciers, fjords; steep cliffs, some of them 300 feet, on either side of the ships; and craggy mountains, up to 7,000 feet above sea level, whose peaks are crowned with eternal mantles of snow. At times, thousand-year-old chunks of ice come crashing down, carrying rocks and trees with them. One of the highlights of the voyage is the arrival at the site of the ancient glaciers, where tourists are treated to refreshments cooled with ice that has existed since before the arrival of the first humans.

The yearly precipitation in Chile ranges from none in parts of the north to some 14 inches in Santiago, and in the southern Central Valley measures up to 200 inches annually; it falls mostly from late May to early September. Northern Chile, at times as devoid of moisture as a lunar landscape, to which it has often been compared, is barren on the surface; vegetation is found only around the few rivers which flow from the Andes seaward, or girding the scattered oases. Sometimes underground water supports life in the desert. The earth below, however, is rich in minerals, especially copper and, importantly until the early twentieth century, nitrate, an essential ingredient in the manufacture of gunpowder and is also a rich fertilizer.

Chile is divided into twelve *regiones* (regions) plus the Región Metropolitana de Santiago (Santiago Metropolitan Region). Formerly, the nation was divided into provinces; the change to regions began during the military government of Augusto Pinochet.

Región I is Tarapacá, in the north, and the historical city of Iquique is its main city. This region has a total population of close to 375,000, 150,000 of whom live in Iquique, which has become a tourist center.

Región II is Antofagasta, its capital the city of the same name. This area has been important for its nitrate, which until the early twentieth century was Chile's most important product. The region's total population is almost identical to Tarapacá's but Antofagasta City is appreciably larger, with some 225,000 inhabitants.

Región III is Atacama; its capital is Copiapó. Until the end of the War of the Pacific (see "History"), Copiapó was the northern border of the nation and the northern terminus of its railroad. The Atacama is the driest desert on earth, with areas that have not recorded any rain for over four centuries. Copiapó has a population of 75,000 out of a total of 200,000 for the entire region.

Región IV is Coquimbo; its capital is the colonial city of La Serena, one of the most beautiful small cities in the country. It is popular with both permanent residents and vacationers. It has a pleasant, mild climate all year and has preserved its colonial past very well. This region has approximately a half million inhabitants; La Serena has 125,000.

Región V is Valparaíso, third largest in population in the country. Its capital is Valparaíso, the seat of Chile's legislative government since the early 1990s and the nation's chief port. Many of the country's finest summer resorts are found south and north of the city, and Santiago is accessible by good roads as well as train and bus service. A high-speed magnetic train between Santiago and Valparaíso is currently being considered. This region has a population of around 1.5 million. Viña del Mar, the beautiful seaside resort, is adjacent to Valparaíso and has a population of some 150,000. The combined populations of these two cities form the second largest concentration of people outside of Santiago.

The Metropolitan Region includes the capital city of Santiago and environs. In area it covers only 15,348 square kilometers, but its population exceeds 6 million, most of it in the capital, making it by far the most populous region in the country.

Región VI bears the name of Chile's independence war hero and first president, Libertador (Liberator) General Bernardo O'Higgins. Its capital is Rancagua, with a population of almost 200,000; it was the site of a famous battle in the War for Independence.

Región VII is Maule; its capital is Talca. The region's population is 850,000, of which 180,000 are in the capital. There are those who think of Talca the way some Americans think of Boston (that is, a center of culture), especially those who live there. There is a sort of tongue-in-cheek comment, and often an accompanying T-shirt, that states boldly, "París, Londres, y Talca" (Paris, London, and Talca), thus placing this Chilean city in the elite company of those two European centers of culture.

Región VIII is Bío-Bío, population 1.7 million; its capital is Concepción, with some 325,000 inhabitants, making this city Chile's second in population after Santiago. The capital is the site of one of Chile's best universities, the Universidad de Concepción, long known for its liberalism and opposition to government intrusion into its independence. To the north of Concepción is the port of Talcahuano, the base for much of Chile's navy.

Región IX is La Araucanía (literally, where the Araucanians live) with a population of 800,000. Its capital, Temuco, is one of southern Chile's major cities. It has a population of 250,000 and, as the region's name implies, has the largest concentration of Chile's original inhabitants, the Araucanians (Mapuches).

Región X is Los Lagos (The Lakes); its capital is the port of Puerto Montt, long known as the southern terminus for the railroad, and the last city of "mainland" Chile. The area south of Puerto Montt is composed of land on the east and fjords surrounded by innumerable islands on the west, all the way to the end of the continent. Los Lagos is aptly named, for some of Chile's most beautiful lakes are found not far from Puerto Montt, among them Llanquihue, with the majestic Osorno volcano on its eastern shore, and Lake Todos los Santos (All Saints Lake), with the Osorno on its western end. Many tourists travel on Todos los Santos to the Argentine border and beyond, sailing into Lake Nahuel Huapí, to reach the Argentine resort of San Carlos de Bariloche.

Región XI has the long official name of Aisén del General Carlos Ibáñez del Campo. It is named in honor of General Ibáñez, who was twice president of Chile, the last time from 1952 to 1958, and was instrumental in encouraging the growth of an area of the country that was sparsely populated. Aisén has a population of only some 90,000; its capital, Coihaique, has around 35,000.

Región XII, Magallanes, the southernmost in the country, includes the area of Antarctica claimed by Chile. Its population is 165,000, most of whom (125,000) live in the region's capital, Punta Arenas which, located at the 53rd parallel, is one of the southernmost cities in the world.

DEMOGRAPHY

Chile's population hovers at slightly over 15 million, with a growth rate approximating 1.6 percent, lower than all other Latin American nations save Argentina and Uruguay (1.2 percent and 0.6 percent, respectively). The majority of its inhabitants are in the Central Valley, where Santiago is located. This city has a population of over 5 million and is growing rapidly, mostly as a result of the continuing migration of people from other areas of the country. Other major cities are Valparaíso (Valley of Paradise), the main port, around 80 miles west of the capital, with 325,000 inhabitants; the attractive resort of Viña del Mar (Vineyard of the Sea), only 6 miles from Valparaíso; and Concepción, 300 miles to the southwest, also with over 300,000 inhabitants. A few cities in the arid north have growing populations as well, among them Antofagasta, with some 225,000, and Iquique, with 150,000. The southern terminus of the rail system is the port of Puerto Montt, with a population of 130,000; it is 600 miles south of Santiago. The windy city of Punta Arenas, 900 miles further south, as the crow flies, is sparsely populated, numbering slightly less than that of Iquique.

Life expectancy has reached seventy-two years for males and seventy-eight for females and continues to rise, while infant mortality has dropped to some 10.4 deaths per 1,000 live births (the U.S. rate is 9 per 1,000). The rate of literacy is nearly 96 percent, comparing favorably with Argentina, Costa Rica, Uruguay, and the United States. The composition of the population by age groups is as follows: 39.7 percent are up to nineteen years of age, 33.6 percent are twenty to thirty-nine; 20.6 percent are forty to sixty-four; and 6.1 percent are sixty-five or older.

Education consists of four levels: preschool, up to the age of six; basic or primary; middle; and postsecondary or university. Primary is free and obligatory for children from the age of six through fourteen, and is divided into two cycles. The first four years offer a general education; during the second four years, students focus on more specialized studies. The middle level creates further specialization by directing students into one of the following areas of concentration: scientific-humanistic studies, technical-professional studies, commercial studies, or industrial and agricultural studies.

In 1981, a significant transformation began to occur across the entire spectrum of education. State universities were restructured and many private institutions were created. A large part of state basic and middle education was moved to the control of local municipalities. Parallel to these changes, an intensive literacy program had begun in 1980; the end result was that the rate of illiteracy was reduced by 10 percent from the level in 1970.

ETHNIC GROUPS

The ethnic composition of Chile's population reflects the historical migrations that began thousands of years ago, when the first native populations began to come in successive waves from the north, and ended with the arrival of non-native people, mostly from Europe and the Middle East, between the second half of the nineteenth century and the middle of the twentieth. All of these mixes have enriched the ethnic makeup of present-day Chileans.

The first Spaniards who came to America were almost all male. It was not until serious attempts at colonization arose that the first women began to emigrate. Thus, the first race created in the New World, what the early twentieth-century Mexican essayist José Vasconcelos referred to as the "cosmic race" in his work of the same name (1925), was the result of the crossing of two races: white, male Spaniards and Native American females. At first, almost all these children were born out of wedlock. The native inhabitants of Chile were not as numerous as those of the Andean regions of present-day Peru, Bolivia, and Ecuador, and of the Central American and Mexican highlands. Thus, *mestizaje*, the blending of the races, produced biracial people who were more equally balanced in their ethnic makeup than was the case in the other countries just mentioned.

Successive groups of Europeans, especially from Spain but also from other countries, continued to immigrate to Chile in small but significant numbers during the early nineteenth century. During the second half of that century, the government of Chile encouraged and supported the emigration of immigrants, many from Germany. Thousands came to Chile, especially to the area between Santiago and Puerto Montt, and established colonies modeled after the areas from which they had come. Today, their descendants continue to make up a significant proportion of the residents of the lake regions of the south, and many German names are found in cities such as Puerto Montt, Puerto Varas, and Valdivia. A monument in Puerto Montt honors the first German settlers to arrive in Chile in the 1840s.

In the nineteenth and twentieth centuries there has also been immigration to Chile from the Middle East, especially from the Christian communities within Lebanon, Syria, and Palestine. These people blended into Chilean society, becoming respected members of the business community and the government. Many of the new arrivals saw the spelling of their names altered because of officials' difficulty with their unusual names. Nevertheless, most still bear names that reflect their Middle Eastern heritage. The contributions made by these various immigrants have greatly enriched Chilean society and culture.

The first Palestinians arrived in Chile during the second half of the nineteenth century. The Ottoman Empire was beginning to lose the Crimean War against England in the Balkans, and the Turks started to recruit Palestinians, Syrians, and Lebanese, especially those who were Christians, as soldiers. Many parents, wanting to keep their children from being inducted into the Turkish armed forces, began to send them overseas, especially to North and South America. Since their ports of embarkation were under Turkish control, the new arrivals were, and still continue to be referred to, informally and incorrectly, as *turcos* (Turks). Another great influx of Middle Easterners arrived in 1948, after the creation of the state of Israel.

Some of these Palestinians, especially those from the area of Bethlehem, were from highly educated families, and at first dissociated themselves from those who arrived in Chile with less education. Later, this social segregation began to disappear, and today it is a distant memory. Names such as Yarur, Said, Abuhomor, and Aguad today feature prominently in Chilean business, social, and political circles.

Other Europeans who have blended into the Chilean society have come from the former Yugoslavia; they are mostly Croatians who arrived before the middle of the century and who have settled mainly in the southernmost regions of the country. According to the census of 1992, 135,000 persons are Croatian natives or descendants of Croatian immigrants; in Punta Arenas, one out of every four inhabitants is of Croatian descent. Chile's Croatian population is the fifth largest in the world. Families from the former Yugoslavia are again being welcomed to Chile, irrespective of whether they are Serbs, Bosnians, or Croatians, although those in the last group will be more easily absorbed because many Croatians have already settled successfully in the country. During the Kosovo crisis, the government of Chile welcomed refugees from that embattled province of the former Yugoslavia.

Native Americans, mostly Araucanians, in the south of the country, especially around the city of Temuco, and the relatively few Aymarás, in the northern areas bordering Bolivia, are said to number perhaps 400,000 to 500,000, some 3 percent of the population. The balance is equally divided between European and Middle Eastern descendants and mestizos (the product of white and Indian). The homogeneity of the population, the hardiness of the native inhabitants and of the immigrants who settled the land, and the political stability that has characterized Chile, have produced a nation whose middle class is significant and more successful in economic terms than those in most other Latin American states.

CHILE, CHILEAN

Since a book devoted to the culture and customs of Chile will, of necessity, frequently use the adjective "Chilean" and the noun "Chile," there is no better beginning for what follows than showing how both the adjective of nationality and the country's name are pronounced, especially since they are so often mispronounced even by those who are supposedly experts in Latin American studies.

Chile is pronounced, "chil'e," with the stress on the first syllable, pronounced like "chill," and the "e" sounding like the "ee" of "see." Another pronunciation parallels the actual one in Spanish, for the "e" sounds like that letter in the word "ebb"; the stress remains on the first syllable. "Chilean" is pronounced, "Chil'e-an"; the stress is on the first syllable; the "e" has the sound of that letter in the word "see" and the "an" sounds like the word "Anne."

CURRENCY

The unit of currency in Chile is the *peso* (written as $1). The exchange rate during most of 1999 stayed around 500 pesos to the U.S. dollar. Its relative value, measured against the dollar, has varied considerably in the past, depending on the rate of inflation. In 1960, the peso reached an exchange rate of approximately 1,000 pesos = U.S. $1.00. Partly in an effort to change the inflationary mind-set of the nation, the Chilean government dropped the peso as its unit of currency and created the *escudo* (E^0), making it equal to 1,000 old pesos. For a time, this new unit of currency was maintained roughly equal to the dollar. By 1962, however, the pressures of inflation caused its value to begin to drop, and it continued to decline throughout the rest of the 1960s. During the turbulent economic years of the Popular Unity government of Salvador Allende (1970–1973), the inflationary pressures became so great that by 1973, the *escudo* had dropped as low as 3,000 to the dollar. In the first years of the Pinochet government, the peso was brought back. Inflation remained fairly high during the 1970s and early 1980s, then began to move downward to rates that had been unknown in Chile for many years. The present exchange rate is stationary enough that the peso is considered to be a stable and reliable currency.

Coins exist in values of 1, 5, 10, and 100 pesos. The first two are seldom used due to their relatively insignificant face value; the 10 and 100 peso coins are common, especially the latter. Like many other people in the world, Chileans do not concern themselves very much with loose change, especially the lower denominations. Thus, a common practice when paying for something is to round the price to the nearest "significant" amount. Thus, when change due to a customer is between 1 peso and 10 or 20 pesos, it is common to disregard the coins involved and to say, "No importa" (It doesn't matter).

Until perhaps the early 1950s, when the peso had relatively more value in relation to the dollar, it was further subdivided into 100 *centavos*, or cents. There were two coins in wide circulation, the 20 centavo piece and the 50 centavo piece. Children could purchase one bite-sized piece of candy for 20 centavos and could ride to school for as little as 60 centavos. The 20 centavo coin was familiarly known as *chaucha*. Today, the only thing left of that coin in the memory of some Chileans is the expression "*No tengo ni una chaucha*," literally, "I haven't even one *chaucha*," or "I'm flat broke."

Bills exist in denominations of 500, 1,000, 5,000, and 10,000 pesos. The first is somewhat hard to find in a typical billfold or purse; most people use 100 peso coins in its place. The 1,000 peso bill is the most common unit of currency, and many sale items have that magic number as their cost. Many Chileans use the term *luca* for the 1,000 peso bill, today worth a bit over U.S. $2.00. Many years ago, one *luca* had a significant value; inflation has changed that, of course. Bills in denominations of 5,000 and 10,000 pesos (roughly U.S. $10–$20) are commonly used but sometimes hard to find.

More and more, Chileans are moving toward the use of credit cards, and many use personal checks. It is fairly common for restaurant customers to pay their bills with personal checks rather than with cash or plastic.

CHILEAN SPANISH

Spanish is the official language of Chile. The Spanish word for the language is *español*. In Chile, as well as in the rest of the countries of the Southern Cone (Argentina, Uruguay, Paraguay), and in Peru and Ecuador as well, people prefer to say *castellano* rather than *español*. Thus, to say "Do you speak Spanish?," one normally says "*¿Habla castellano?*" rather than "*¿Habla español?*" The terms *español* and *castellano* have come to be synonymous in the Hispanic world, but deep in the Chilean's subconscious mind, the question "¿Habla español?" still seems to ask, "Do you speak Spanish (like a Spaniard)?" Still, for those who have a fair amount of knowledge of the Spanish language, both questions elicit the same response.

A best-selling book titled *How to Survive in the Chilean Jungle*, written by John Brennan, an American, and Alvaro Taboada, a Chilean, appeared in Chile in 1996, and became an instant hit. Brennan had planned to spend five months in Chile, with the intention of improving his knowledge of Spanish, before entering graduate school in the United States. In Santiago, he met and became friends with Taboada. The American's planned five-month stay stretched to two years as he and Taboada began to collaborate on a book that would attempt to clarify the "jungle" of Chilean Spanish for the uninitiated tourist.

How to Survive in the Chilean Jungle obviously has nothing to do with geographical topography but much to say about what makes the Spanish spoken in Chile a unique expression of Chilean culture. It is replete with terms from Spanish, Indian languages, English, German, Italian, and even Serbo-Croatian, reflecting Chileans' varied ancestry. The native speaker of Spanish who travels to Chile has much less difficulty than the non-Spanish speaker who has learned the language in school. Still, the "jungle" that Brennan and Taboada are referring to is not as impenetrable as the uninitiated reader might believe. The book is written with a great deal of tongue-in-cheek humor. Something similar could be, and probably has been, done in other Spanish-speaking countries. The book is a must for anyone who wishes to enjoy and begin to understand the singularity of Chile's brand of Spanish. Its instant success vindicates the belief that Chilean Spanish, while certainly a part of the language given birth to by Spain, still has unique qualities that bear study and appreciation.

At the end of the book is "The Spanish of Chile," an appendix that gives examples of regionalisms with which any Chilean is familiar. They provide the outsider with cultural tidbits that will make a stay there more fruitful and enjoyable. They also make natives smile broadly as they recognize those bits of culture with which they have grown up. Although a knowledge of Spanish makes comprehension or usage of some of the expressions easier, readers without such a familiarity can still appreciate the uniqueness of the way in which Chileans communicate with each other.

THE ESMERALDA

The name "Esmeralda" stands out in the Chilean national consciousness. Several ships have borne that name since the early years of the republic, and mention of this illustrious name brings to mind the country's military deeds since the times of O'Higgins, as well as the image of the last ship to bear the name, the training ship *Esmeralda* which is part of Chile's navy.

The current *Esmeralda* is the sixth ship to bear the name since 1818, when Captain Jorge O'Brien, commander of the nation's first naval force, boarded and died aboard the Spanish frigate *Esmeralda* in a vain attempt to capture it. Two years later, Admiral Lord Thomas Cochrane (see "History") captured the ship for Chile.

In 1854, a second ship bearing the name was built in England according to the specifications of Captain Roberto Simpson and Admiral Blanco Encalada. That ship saw action during Chile's brief war against Spain in 1865. During that conflict the ship's commander, Captain Juan Williams, captured the Spanish corvette *Covadonga*, which later saw action against Peru during the War of the Pacific.

On May 21, 1879, the *Esmeralda* and the *Covadonga* faced a superior force of two ships of the Peruvian navy. The *Esmeralda* was sunk, but the *Covadonga* performed a daring maneuver that, in effect, neutralized the Peruvian battleship, *Independencia*, for some time.

In 1942, Spain ordered the construction of a sailing ship to replace its training ship *Sebastián de Elcano*, named after the first man to circumnavigate the world. The construction was not completed, and the Chilean navy was offered the ship as partial payment for debts that Spain had incurred with Chile during the Spanish Civil War (1936–1939). The ship was completed according to Chilean specifications and was launched in May 1953. It was officially handed over to Chile on June 15, 1954, and has served as the nation's training ship ever since.

THE SEASONS

Since Chile is south of the Equator, its four seasons occur at the exact opposites times from what North Americans and Europeans experience. Certainly, the first Spanish travelers to the southern latitudes of the American continent realized that the weather they were experiencing did not match what they had left behind on the Iberian Peninsula. Their experience in the New World was not totally unexpected, however, since travelers who had rounded the Cape of Good Hope had noticed that the period from December to March was much warmer than the months of June, July, and August.

Summer in Chile officially begins on December 21 and ends on March 21. Autumn begins on March 21 and runs through June 21, at which time winter begins and continues until September 21. Spring completes the cycle by lasting from September 21 until December 21. The largest concentration of Chileans inhabit the area from just north of Santiago to Región X, some 600 miles south of the capital. For them there are four distinct seasons with the expected changes of climate.

Winter in the Central Valley, where Santiago is located, tends to be cool, with temperatures normally ranging from a low of 0° C (32° F) to a high of 18° C (65° F). The average rainfall of some 30 cm. (12 in. a year) tends to occur mostly during June, July, and August. Snow is rare in the Valley but common at the higher altitudes. Rainfall, and sometimes snow, increases dramatically from Santiago southward, reaching up to 500 cm. (200 in.) south of Puerto Montt. Precipitation from the Central Valley northward decreases as well, with the city of Arica, on the border with Peru, receiving an average of 2.5 cm. (1 in.) per year. As was mentioned earlier, the Atacama Desert, in Chile's north, has areas where rainfall has not been recorded for more than 400 years.

In central Chile the summer is warm and dry, and rain is rare, less common than in the winter as one moves south to Puerto Montt. Temperatures around Santiago range from a pleasantly cool 10° C (50° F) at night, to an average high of 29° C (85° F) during the warmest part of the day, although higher temperatures do occur. The low humidity, however, tends to make the summer quite bearable. Most homes are not air-conditioned because they have been built to withstand the heat buildup during the day. By late afternoon temperatures begin to drop to very comfortable levels, and people can sit outdoors on patios or terraces, or they can go for strolls.

Schools begin the academic year in March and continue until a few days before the Christmas holidays. Usually in July, students have a two-week winter vacation. Many universities now divide their academic years into a fall session that runs from March to July and a spring term that runs from July through December. One very obvious benefit of this correlation between seasons and academic year is that students can measure their education by calendar years, rather than from the fall of one year through the spring of the next, as is commonly done in the northern hemisphere.

The seasonal variation in Chile makes for a citizenry that has an outlook similar to that of Europeans and North Americans, especially when contrasted with those who live in the tropical areas of the world, where temperature variation is minimal and where there tend to be two seasons, the dry and the wet. There is a certain renewal brought about by the changing of the seasons—the falling of the leaves in the fall, the sometimes cold rain during the winter, the new growth of flowers and leaves in the spring, and the warmth of the sun in the summer. Chileans tend to be somewhat Phoenix-like as a result of the seasonal changes, and this might serve to explain their uniqueness among their Latin confreres.

HISTORY

Conquest and Discovery

Up to this point, the most widely accepted theory relating to the origin of the first human inhabitants of the American continent is that they probably came from Asia over a land bridge spanning the Bering Strait between Siberia and Alaska. They slowly migrated southward through what today are the countries of North, Central, and South America, until they could go no further. They had reached what today are Chile and Argentina.

The first written accounts of the history of Chile known to us are the letters or other communications written by the Spanish conquistadors who first arrived there in the 1530s. But there is more than sufficient evidence that the original inhabitants of Chile had arrived from 10,000 to 25,000 years ago. When Ferdinand Magellan, struggling to reach the Moluccas, a group of islands that are today part of Indonesia, came upon the strait which was later to bear his name, he was unaware that the land around him had been inhabited for thousands of years.

In 1536, when Spanish conquistador Diego de Almagro arrived in the Valley of Copiapó, at the 27th parallel and originally the northern border of Chile, the native population was composed of diverse tribes that were commonly referred to as Mapuches, which means "People of the Land," according to some, and "Men from the East," according to others. They were members of the Guaraní tribe who had moved south from Brazil, then over the Argentine pampas, and finally across the Andes, reaching the Mapocho River, which bisects present-day Santiago. Moving farther south, they mostly settled the area known today as Araucanía, between the Bío-Bío and Bueno rivers, south of Concepción. Thus, most of them lived in the area now encompassed between Santiago and Puerto Montt. The ethnic term "Araucanians," from the Quechua word *auca*, meaning "indomitable," was given to these natives by the Spaniards. It was a name they deserved, as conquistadors and, later, non-Indian Chileans confirmed.

When the first Spaniards arrived, in the third decade of the sixteenth century, the Araucanians did not live in cities, but in groups made up of several tribes. Each tribe was made up of families who were led by a chief, known as a cacique, who was generally the oldest or the bravest. In times of war, all of the tribes recognized the authority of a supreme leader, the *toqui*.

These native inhabitants engaged in basic agriculture and the raising of animals, as well as fishing and hunting. Among their crops were squash, beans, and corn. For farming, they used hand-made tools such as the trident, stone and wooden shovels, and hoes. Among their weapons were the *maza* (a wooden mace); bows and arrows; the lance, made from the native *coligüe* tree; and *boleadoras*, which consisted of three ropes with wooden balls attached to the ends. These, common also among the natives of Argentina, were thrown to bring down animals and enemies, for they wrapped themselves around the legs and caused them to fall. Later, the Argentine gaucho employed them in similar fashion.

Araucanian women were very adept at weaving and knitting, using the wool from the guanaco, alpaca, and llama (ruminants related to the camel) to produce excellent weavings and bright ponchos, sashes, and headbands. Later, with the coming of the Spaniards, sheep's wool began to be used as well. All of these materials are still employed.

Early in 1540, the Spanish captain don Pedro de Valdivia set out on an arduous voyage from Cuzco, Peru, with 150 soldiers and 1,000 Indian allies, on a long march southward in search of wealth and fame. Valdivia had been born circa 1500 in Villanueva de la Serena, in the province of Extremadura, Spain, the son of impoverished middle-class parents. He had an education far superior to that of many of his fellow conquistadors, especially the Pizarro brothers, who had just conquered Peru, and Almagro, first their associate and later their foe. Valdivia's associates in Peru looked upon Chile with profound disdain as a result of what they had learned from the soldiers who had accompanied Almagro on his first trip south five years earlier. In spite of their disparaging comments, Valdivia asked Francisco Pizarro for author-

Diorama of the founding of Santiago on February 12, 1541, by Pedro de Valdivia. The site is Huelén Hill, also known as Santa Lucía. The future capital of Chile was named in honor of Spain's patron saint.

ization to conquer and colonize Chile. Pizarro attempted to dissuade his best captain from undertaking the enterprise but acceded before the firm resolution of Valdivia, who spent all of his wealth in organizing the army that accompanied him.

On December 13, 1540, Valdivia reached the valley of the Mapocho River and camped next to Huelén Hill, which he renamed Santa Lucía, for the saint honored on that day. On February 12, 1541, Valdivia founded the city of Santiago de Nueva Extremadura, in dual honor of Spain's patron saint, St. James, and of the area of Spain from which he had come. Valdivia assumed the role of military commander and governor of the new colony.

While Valdivia organized and fortified the new colony, the Araucanians gathered together in an attempt to drive out the foreign invaders. Since there was no consensus as to who would lead the struggle against the Spaniards, the caciques met to choose their *toqui*. As narrated in Ercilla's poem *La Araucana*, a feat of strength was chosen as the method to select the leader. A heavy tree trunk was to be carried on each candidate's shoulders for as long as he could bear it. One cacique, Paicavi, kept it aloft for six hours; another, Elicura, for nine; and yet another, Purén, for twelve. Lincoyán carried it on his shoulders for twenty hours, and felt that his feat would be unequaled. Just as those gathered were about to name him *toqui*, a young brave named Caupolicán stepped forward and hoisted the heavy trunk onto his shoulders. After almost a day and a half, he cast the trunk far away to show that he could have carried it even longer. Colo Colo, the elder whom Ercilla depicts as a classic orator in the manner of Cato, declared Caupolicán the victor and *toqui*. The year was 1553.

Lautaro, a young man who had lived among the Spaniards as a prisoner for nearly a year, escaped his captors and joined his compatriots. In a fiery speech he explained to them some of the military techniques he had learned from the Spaniards, which consisted of attacking the enemy in successive waves until the enemy was exhausted. The Araucanians approved of Lautaro's plans and named him vice *toqui*. Lautaro was twenty years old.

Immediately after having been chosen, Caupolicán had attached the fortified town of Arauco, located on the Gulf of Arauco, almost directly south of Concepción, which was defended by a considerable number of Spaniards. He overwhelmed it and continued on to destroy the fort at Tucapel, some ninety miles due east of Arauco. Valdivia learned of this latest Indian uprising while in Concepción, but believing it to be of little significance, took only some fifty horsemen to repel it.

Valdivia arrived at the site of the fort at Tucapel with the original fifty men and an additional ten who had joined him along the way. There, he was attacked by successive waves of Araucanians and, in spite of the Spaniards' military training and valor, none of them escaped alive. Lautaro, brilliant general that he had become, had closed off all avenues of escape.

Valdivia was captured and taken before Lautaro and Caupolicán. He asked that his life be spared, but as the caciques deliberated, another leader, Leucotón, struck him on the nape of the neck with his *maza*, killing him. Valdivia, the first governor of Chile, was dead at the age of fifty-six, almost thirteen years after his founding of Santiago.

The death of Valdivia sowed fear among the inhabitants of the colony. The new governor, don Francisco de Villagra, left Concepción the year after Valdivia's death and went out to challenge Lautaro. Lautaro defeated him at Marihueñu and then crossed the Bío-Bío River in order to attack Concepción. Its residents evacuated the city, and the Indians sacked and burned their homes.

Lautaro, heartened by his success, conceived the bold idea of expelling the foreign invaders from all of Chile. In 1556, he crossed the Maule River on his way to Santiago while Caupolicán moved south toward the cities of

Imperial and Valdivia. Such was the fear among the capital's citizens that there was a plan to abandon it and move north to La Serena, or even to leave Chile and return to Peru.

Troops under Pedro de Villagra, brother of the governor, attempted to stop the advancing Araucanians. The opposing sides met at the edge of the Mataquito River, and in the skirmish Lautaro was victorious. The coming of winter, however, gave respite to the defeated Spaniards, for Lautaro returned north to await the advent of spring. He camped again at the edge of the Mataquito River. Villagra surrounded Lautaro's army and, in a daring maneuver, had Indian allies dress like Spaniards and pretend to be withdrawing toward Santiago. Lautaro, advised that the enemy was leaving, relaxed and rested. At the same time, an Indian betrayed him by leading the Spanish toward Lautaro's camp. Lautaro, mortally wounded, died in his wife's arms. It was the morning of April 29, 1557. His head was stuck on a pike and taken to Santiago to be displayed.

Lautaro and Caupolicán are treasured figures in Chilean history. A third Araucanian leader, Galvarino, has also left a deep imprint in the minds of Chileans. This warrior was captured in Lagunillas, a place west of Santiago not far from the coast. The governor ordered that his hands be severed and that he be freed so that the enemy might be terrified by this punishment inflicted upon those who rebelled. The story goes that when the moment arrived for Galvarino's torture, he calmly placed his left hand upon the tree trunk. As soon as he had seen it fall away from his wrist, he had placed the right one there without any display of pain. After having both his hands cut off, he placed his neck on the spot so as to be decapitated. When his torturers refused, he displayed great indignation and moved off, promising revenge. In 1557, the Indians, emboldened by Galvarino's torture, attacked the Spaniards in a district called Millarapue. Galvarino was taken prisoner once again, and this time he was sentenced to be hanged from a tree. The poet Ercilla, impressed by the Indian's valor, made every effort to keep him from being executed, arguing that he had seen Galvarino changing sides and joining the Spanish troops. Galvarino, displaying his mutilated arms, until then covered by a shawl, refused Ercilla's offer to commute his death sentence and said that he only wished that he could tear his enemies apart with his teeth. The sentence was quickly carried out.

In 1557, don García Hurtado de Mendoza, a youth of twenty-two, was named governor of Chile by his father, the viceroy of Peru, and was sent south to his new post. Accompanying him was Alonso de Ercilla y Zúñiga, who wrote *La Araucana* as he fought alongside the new governor. The tide began to turn in favor of the Spaniards, although the struggle against the Indians continued until the last quarter of the nineteenth century.

While don García explored the south, Caupolicán planned an assault on Cañete, but before this could be done, he was betrayed by an Indian named Andresillo. His attack failed, and he was captured by the Spaniards. His execution is the stuff of legend and, along with his prowess on the field of battle, has earned him an exalted place in the pantheon of Chilean heroes.

Captain Alonso de Reinoso, commandant of the fortified town of Cañete, condemned Caupolicán to die by impalement. This cruel torture consisted of forcing the victim to sit on a sharpened wooden stake which was erected on a platform. Caupolicán watched the executioner, an African, approach him to force him onto the stake. Unable to bear the ignominy of being forced to sit on the instrument of torture by a slave, Caupolicán kicked the executioner off the platform and calmly proceeded to sit on the stake without assistance or force. Near the top of Santa Lucía Hill, in Santiago, there now stand two statues; one honors Pedro de Valdivia; the other, Caupolicán. The latter's statue shows him in an arrogant pose, as a symbol of an indomitable race. The animosity that still exists toward the conquistadors in Mexico, where no monument to Cortés is to be found, does not exist for the conquerors of Chile, though some have noted that Caupolicán's statue stands a bit higher on the hill than does that of the first governor. A magnificent monument to Ercilla, the poet/soldier who documented it all, is to be found at the entrance to Cousiño Park in Santiago.

Under García Hurtado de Mendoza, the conquest of Chile, though incomplete, was advanced considerably. Under his orders, Juan de Ladrillero took possession of the Strait of Magellan in 1557, and extended Chile's claim considerably to the south. An expedition under Pedro del Castillo was sent across the Andes, and the cities of Mendoza and San Juan were founded. Both of them, however, were later claimed by Argentina and today are part of that nation.

In 1561, King Philip II of Spain named don Francisco de Villagra the new governor of Chile. Hurtado de Mendoza left for Peru, where he later became viceroy of New Castile. The end of don García's government marks the final stage of the Conquest and is considered the beginning of the colonial period, which lasted until 1810.

The Colonial Period (1541–1810)

At the beginning of the colonial period, Chilean territory began at Copiapó, some 500 miles north of the capital, and extended to the Strait of

Magellan in the south. From west to east, it took in the province of Tucumán, and almost all of Patagonia. (Tucumán and most of Patagonia are now part of Argentina.) In 1554, Charles V gave the colony the official name of Kingdom of Chile, with the intention of making his son, don Felipe (later Philip II), king of the distant country, thus facilitating his marriage to Mary Tudor, heir to the English throne. Chile remained a kingdom until 1778, when Charles III, the Bourbon king of Spain, made it a captaincy under the Viceroyalty of New Castile (Peru). In 1563, Tucumán was separated from the Kingdom of Chile; it later became part of the Viceroyalty of Buenos Aires.

The Chilean colony was administered by a governor who also held the title of captain general of the army and who was appointed by the king of Spain. Thirty-five such governors presided until independence was declared in the second decade of the nineteenth century. In the early 1600s, Philip III instituted the Laws of Indies, which regulated even the most minor daily activities of all those who lived in the colony. Since an important function of these laws was to ensure that government officials carried out their duties according to the law, and that the indigenous population was not maltreated, at least their purpose was somewhat altruistic, though actual practice did not always match theory.

Chile and the other Spanish territories in the New World were considered, at least officially, to be an integral part of the mother country and, thus, not colonies. A great fear of the Spanish Crown was that each of these territories, as much due to its great distance from the Iberian Peninsula as to the independent spirit of its citizens, would begin to develop separatist tendencies, especially among those born in America. As the numbers of those born in Chile increased, these fears increased proportionately. In order to maintain a strict control over such tendencies, the Crown kept the government in the hands of Spaniards born in the Iberian Peninsula. Thus, a gap began to develop between the *peninsulares* (those born in Spain) and the *criollos* (those born in America). The Laws of Indies prohibited Spain's leaders from acquiring property, conducting business, and forming close friendships with those born in Chile. Marriage had to take place outside the country. The resentments between *peninsulares* and *criollos* grew in intensity, and by the early 1800s it contributed greatly to the wars of independence which separated Chile from Spain in 1818.

Chilean settlements continued to expand from the late 1500s through the end of the 1700s. Castro, on the island of Chiloé, south of Puerto Montt, was founded in 1563. Several cities located south of Santiago, among them Los Angeles, Rancagua, and Curicó, were founded between 1740 and 1745. Although skirmishes with the Araucanians continued sporadically until the

1880s, such settlements took on a more permanent character than had Valdivia, Concepción, and even Santiago during the first years of the Conquest, when periodic attacks by the Indians sometimes destroyed these cities almost completely.

Indian attacks were not the only dangers that the settlers had to face. There were frequent naval expeditions carried out by corsairs, privateers who often acted with the consent of the English and Dutch monarchs, traditional enemies of the Spanish Crown, as well as by pirates, adventurers who were motivated solely by personal greed. Since the majority of the corsairs were Protestants, Spanish Catholics saw their forays as both criminal acts of war and as God's punishment, at the hands of heretics, for Spanish actions both real and perceived.

Sir Francis Drake was perhaps the best known of the corsairs. Astutely using Magellan's 1520 discovery of the passageway, Drake moved north through the strait and, arriving in Valparaíso, took possession of a ship laden with leather and gold that was bound for Callao, the main port of the Viceroyalty of New Castile. On his way to Callao from Valparaíso, he unsuccessfully attacked the city of La Serena, some 290 miles to the north. He later raided many other Spanish possessions and returned to England, where he was knighted by Queen Elizabeth I. As a result of his travels, Drake became the second sailor to circumnavigate the world.

A fortuitous and interesting event that ties Chile to British literature was the discovery made by Juan Fernández, a little-known Spanish pilot, of a small archipelago some 400 miles off the coast of Valparaíso. While returning to Chile from Peru in 1574, he sailed west at approximately the 34th parallel and landed on a small island where he was fascinated with its exotic vegetation composed of ferns and other native plants, and air permeated by the odor of sandalwood. He soon became aware that he had chanced upon one of a group of three uninhabited islands; they were later named Santa Clara, Más Afuera, and Más a Tierra. The last, the closest to the South American mainland, became famous after having provided asylum to the Scottish sailor Alexander Selkirk, supposed prototype for Daniel Defoe's *Robinson Crusoe* (1719). In 1966, Más a Tierra and Más Afuera were officially given the names Robinson Crusoe and Alejandro Selkirk, respectively. Santa Clara maintains its original name to the present day. Selkirk was abandoned on Más a Tierra in 1703 by a corsair named Stradling. There he lived for more than four years, among his only possessions a rifle and a hatchet, left behind by the corsairs. In 1709, Selkirk was rescued by other corsairs, who were surprised to find a type of ape-man who spoke to them in English.

One of the most distinguished governors that Chile had during the colonial period was Ambrosio O'Higgins. Born in Ireland in 1720, O'Higgins was educated in Spain, traveled to Peru, and there worked as a peddler. In 1762 he arrived in Concepción, where he offered his services to the colony constructing roads. So greatly did he distinguish himself in the services that he rendered the state and so greatly did he rise in the estimation of his superiors that he was first named mayor of Concepción, then governor of Chile (1788–1796), and finally, viceroy of Peru. He died in 1801, in Lima. His fame rests as much on his own accomplishments as on the fact that he was the father of Bernardo O'Higgins, one of the illustrious leaders of Chile's independence from Spain and first president of the new nation.

The Wars of Independence (1810–1818)

The colonial period in most of Spanish America began with the arrival of Columbus in 1492 and ended between 1810 and 1824, when all but Cuba and Puerto Rico began and completed their quest for political independence. The original thirteen colonies that composed the United States, by contrast, were under the control of several European countries, mainly Great Britain, from 1609 through 1776, at which time they began their struggle for political independence.

The reasons for Chile's move toward independence mirror those that led the rest of the Spanish colonies to seek to break their ties with Spain. There had been a growing antagonism between the native-born *criollos* and the peninsular Spaniards who controlled the political lives of the former and maintained a strict social and economic distance between themselves and their American cousins. As pointed out earlier, the Spanish Crown supported this separation for obvious reasons: fear that if the colonists achieved the economic and social benefits that consistently accrued to the peninsulars, they would begin to supplant the latter in positions of political power. Since the *criollos* had already bonded with the land in which they had been born, their allegiance might be more to Chile than to the mother country. This very separation, however, had been slowly but irreversibly leading to a realization by the native-born Americans that in order for them to share in the benefits enjoyed by the Spaniards, they would need to secure at least some degree of legal separation from Spain.

After more than 300 years of life as colonists, neither independent nor slave, the *criollos* had begun to feel that they were neither fish nor fowl. At the same time, however, and in the tradition of their peninsular cousins, they also generally honored their long tradition of allegiance to the Spanish Crown. As expected, they were unsure of the degree of separation they desired from the strict control that Spain had been exercising for so long. By the end of the eighteenth century, the colonists were essentially beginning to separate into four groups. First, there were those who wished to maintain allegiance to Spain. They felt that their bond should not be broken. The other factions shared a common desire for independence to some degree: at times they were united, but often they were at odds as a result of their diverging goals.

An early attempt at independence for Chileans was led by Antonio Gramusset, Antonio Berney, and José Antonio Rojas; the first two were of French nationality; the third was an influential member of Chile's colonial society. In 1780, the three conspired to establish Chile as an independent republic with the backing of the colony's leading *criollos*. They were betrayed, and the Spanish authorities exiled the Frenchmen to Peru but freed the Chilean, fearful of arousing the ire of the *criollos*. The short-lived, unsuccessful attempt became known as "The Conspiracy of the Three Antonios." In 1808, Pedro Ramón Arriagada, a town councillor of Chillán, and Fray Rosauro Acuña, the hospital's prior, were arrested in that southern city and accused of propagating emancipationist ideas. They were taken to Santiago, where they were kept under strict vigilance.

The last governor of the colonial regime was Francisco Antonio García Carrasco, a military man who assumed his duties in 1808. His administrative ineptitude contributed greatly to the events that soon followed.

Some of the external causes that led to the break between Chile and Spain proved to be of paramount importance, for they not only provided what was at first seen as a legal reason for the colonists to seek a separation but also created a diversion for Spain that, for some time evened the playing field or, more appropriately, the battlefield.

The French Revolution of 1789 had proclaimed the principles of liberty, equality, and fraternity. The writings of the French philosophers Montesquieu, Voltaire, and Rousseau, among others, had greatly impressed many of the thinkers of Spanish America. The works of Francisco de Miranda, one of the precursors of Venezuelan independence, were well known to other Spanish American patriots.

The French, under the leadership of Napoleon Bonaparte, invaded the Iberian Peninsula in 1808. The Spanish king, Charles IV, and his son Ferdinand (later Ferdinand VII), had been spirited out of their country and were being kept under house arrest by the invading forces. Napoleon placed his brother Joseph on the Spanish throne, and Spanish nationalism led to an uprising against the invaders, an event dramatically depicted by Francisco de Goya in his painting *The Third of May*. History provided Spanish American patriots a political excuse to seek a separation from Spain: their allegiance had been to Spain, and Spain was under the control of a foreign power.

In the crucial year of 1810, conspiracies were rampant in Chile. When Governor García Carrasco ordered the arrest of three pro-independence *criollos*, José Antonio Rojas, Juan Antonio Ovalle, and Bernardo Vera y Pintado, the populace rose up in rebellion against the measure, demanding their immediate release. The governor, fearing the consequences of this arrest, revoked the order, but by that time, the first two had been put aboard a ship bound for Lima. Vera y Pintado remained behind, due to illness.

Faced by growing opposition, García Carrasco resigned from office on July 16, 1810, and turned over his post to Mateo de Toro y Zambrano, count of La Conquista, a wealthy Chilean born in 1727. In his professional life, Toro y Zambrano had served the colony as mayor and *corregidor* (magistrate) of Santiago and as superintendent of the Casa de Moneda (the mint).

When he replaced García Carrasco, Toro y Zambrano was more than eighty years of age and in ill health. Spaniards and *criollos* attempted to sway him toward allegiance to the Crown and independence, respectively. Persuaded, finally, by the independentist side, Toro y Zambrano assembled a *cabildo abierto* (open town meeting) for the purpose of assuring public safety and as a means of creating a forum for discussion of the future of Chile. At first, he hoped to achieve some consensus regarding the best way to preserve Chile under Ferdinand VII, still the goal of many colonists throughout Spanish America.

The assembly met for the first time on September 18, 1810. Present were the members of the *cabildo*, various functionaries and military men, high church officials, and some 300 residents of the city.

After presiding briefly over the assembly, Toro y Zambrano stood, unsteadily, and turning to the secretary, José Gregorio Argomedo, resigned his position as governor and placed any future role for himself in the hands of those present.

Many of those assembled spoke, some in favor of allegiance to Spain, others leaning toward independence from the mother country. The latter overwhelmed the Loyalists, and a government junta was created with Toro y Zambrano as its president and eight other well-known *criollos* as members. At first the contending factions all swore allegiance to the Spanish king during his captivity. The powerful minority that favored independence at the outset hid its motives under this sworn allegiance to the rightful throne of Spain and, in effect, the Council of the Regency in Spain recognized the legitimacy of the junta. Still, September 18 was henceforth celebrated as Chile's independence day.

Toro y Zambrano died in February 1811, and one of the members of the junta, Juan Martínez de Rozas, an attorney, was chosen to lead the rebellion against Spanish rule. Martínez de Rozas began his tenure by gathering troops and purchasing arms. He decreed that henceforth Chile would be free to trade with all nations of the world, and he finalized preparations for the creation of a National Congress that would ultimately replace the junta.

Spanish loyalists, unhappy with the actions of the junta, conspired to bring about its downfall. On April 1, 1811, the day set for the election of the new deputies to the National Congress, Spanish Colonel Tomás de Figueroa rode with his troops onto the main square, prepared to prevent the elections from taking place. Chilean recruits under Colonel Juan de Dios Vial faced the Loyalist troops and, after a brief battle with relatively few casualties, put down the rebellion. Figueroa took refuge in the Convent of Santo Domingo but was removed from there by Martínez de Rozas himself. He was tried, sentenced, and executed by firing squad.

The elections were carried out peacefully after Figueroa's mutiny and, on July 4, 1811, the First National Congress was officially inaugurated. With its opening, the junta of 1810 was dissolved. Three individuals stood out among the forty-two deputies who had been elected: Manuel de Salas, Bernardo O'Higgins, and Manuel Rodríguez. The three went on to lead the radical faction who aspired to total and immediate Chilean independence. The majority, however, were moderates (also known as conservatives), who did not wish to break violently with Spain. The third faction were the reactionaries, the Loyalists who supported the reestablishment of Spanish rule. The conservative majority named an Executive Junta led by three of their members. The radicals, seeing themselves excluded, protested and left the Congress.

Many of the Spanish Americans who joined the struggles against Loyalist domination had fought alongside those in Spain who had risen up against the occupying forces of Napoleon. When they returned to their respective American states, they quickly joined the *criollos* rebelling against the Loyalists in the New World. One of the most outstanding of these returning soldiers was José Miguel Carrera, who had fought with the Hussars of Galicia. Born in Santiago on October 15, 1785, Carrera was a member of one of the country's wealthiest families. His father, Ignacio de la Carrera, had been a vocal member of the Junta of 1810. Soon after hearing of the uprising in Chile, Carrera left Spain and returned to his country of birth to join the patriots. His brothers Juan José and Luis had already joined those forces. José Miguel was proactive and felt that the revolution was in need of quick and definitive reforms. Soon after returning to Chile, he realized that the majority of the members of Congress were resistant to the events that were moving the country toward a complete break with Spain.

On September 4, 1811, accompanied by his brothers Juan José and Luis, Carrera initiated a revolt among some of the troops in Santiago, the first military coup d'état. He expelled seven conservative deputies from Congress and called a new town meeting to elect a new government junta. In Concepción, Martínez de Rozas almost simultaneously created a provincial junta, independent of Santiago. Carrera, meanwhile, was becoming aware that his rebellion had not achieved the results he had expected; many of the influential positions in the government had been occupied by individuals who did not share his aspirations. He instigated a second rebellion and became president of the new junta.

Several events which were hostile to him personally and which had been instigated by supporters of Martínez de Rozas and Congress led Carrera to dissolve Congress by force. He took on complete responsibility for the government. Martínez de Rozas rose up against him but was overwhelmed, captured, and exiled to Mendoza, where he died in 1813.

Carrera led the government throughout 1812, refusing any remuneration for his services. During his dictatorship, the Constitution of 1812 was enacted. A republican form of government was adopted and the national flag and coat of arms were created. Carrera also installed the first printing press and published the first newspaper. He decreed the creation of free schools in any village with more than fifty citizens. He established diplomatic relations with the United States and received the first American diplomatic envoy, Joel Roberts Poinsett.

The period between 1810 and 1814, known as the *Patria Vieja* (Old Fatherland), corresponds to the years when Spain, still under French occupation, was hampered in its efforts to restore absolute Spanish control. As was the case in other New World colonies, Chile experienced both civil strife and progress towards national growth.

The first printing press arrived in Valparaíso toward the end of 1811. It was ordered from the United States by a naturalized American citizen of Swedish descent, Mateo Arnaldo Hoevel, who was living in Santiago and who clearly supported the patriot cause. The advent of the press greatly aided Carrera in his efforts to seek support for the revolution and prestige for his cause in leading it.

On February 13, 1812, Friar Camilo Henriquez, patriot and ally of Carrera, was put in charge of the first newspaper of Chile, *La Aurora de Chile*. Supporters of the revolution were inspired by the publication; the Loyalists looked upon it with great disdain. Although *La Aurora* was a weekly, one-page publication, and obviously lacked impartiality, it provided the populace with important news of the events which were shaping the coming struggle.

There were other significant events in this early period which helped to establish Chile among those nations for which education and literacy were of paramount importance. On August 10, 1813, the year after José Miguel Carrera had been replaced by a government junta under the presidency of Agustín Eyzaguirre, the nation founded the Instituto Nacional by fusing together all existing schools. The National Library was created later that same month, on August 19, using as its base the library of the Real Universidad de San Felipe (Royal University of Saint Philip) and some one hundred books donated by patriots. Both of these institutions were closed by the Spanish government during the Reconquest, which followed the expulsion of Napoleon's troops from the Iberian Peninsula. There is a story that during that period, General José de San Martín (about whom more will be said later), when offered 10,000 pesos in gold to cover personal expenses incurred during his campaign of liberation, accepted the gift and immediately donated it to the Library to further its growth and influence on national education.

Bernardo O'Higgins, the George Washington of Chile, was the son of Ambrosio O'Higgins and Isabel Riquelme. He was born in Chillán on August 20, 1788, and died in Peru in 1842. Sent to school in Peru at the age of ten, he continued his studies in England and returned to Chile at the age of twenty-three in order to take over the Las Canteras hacienda which his father had left to him upon his death. Although the Carreras and O'Higgins families cooperated against the common enemy, the Loyalists, they had more than one falling out. Their differences ultimately led to the deaths of the Carreras and to O'Higgins's assuming leadership of the patriot forces.

In March 1813, Fernando de Abascal, viceroy of Peru, became aware that Carrera had been acting independently of Spain; he sent Brigadier Fernando Parejas with 2,000 men to Santiago to reestablish control of the rebellious forces. He landed in San Vicente and, after occupying Talcahuano and Concepcíon without resistance, marched north toward Santiago. News of the arrival of the Spanish troops caused great alarm among the citizens of the capital. José Miguel Carrera quickly gathered an army and led it to face Parejas. O'Higgins left his hacienda and joined Carrera in Talca, placing himself under Carrera's command. On April 27, 500 patriots surprised the larger Spanish army and forced it to retreat in defeat towards Chillán, where, in May, they settled in for the winter. Instead of renewing his attack on the Loyalists in Chillán, Carrera marched toward Concepción and Talcahuano in an effort to recover those cities for the rebel side. Pareja died in Chillán and was replaced by Juan Francisco Sánchez. By the time Carrera returned to Chillán, the Spaniards had dug in and replenished their provisions. The patriots attacked the Loyalists, but by August 10, lacking the necessities that

Equestrian statue of Chile's first president, Bernardo O'Higgins, in Arica. Near it is another famous site in Chile's history, the Morro, a bluff that Chileans took from Peru during the War of the Pacific.

the latter had gathered, were forced to lift the siege of Chillán, suffering heavy casualties and giving up their earlier advantage.

As the day began on October 17, 1813, divisions led by Carrera and O'Higgins were attacked by the Loyalists at Paso del Roble, on the Itata River, south of Chillán. The rebels fled in disarray, completely surprised by the unexpected attack from the Loyalists; Carrera jumped into the river to escape. In the midst of the confusion, O'Higgins, a bullet wound in his leg, rallied the panicked rebels with an exhortation to fight and turned imminent defeat into victory after three hours of bitter fighting.

Carrera's military prestige was weakened considerably by these events. In November 1813, he turned over his command to O'Higgins. The seeds of enmity, however, had been sowed. José Miguel Carrera and his brother Luis left Santiago and, while attempting to leave the country, were apprehended by Loyalist troops and imprisoned in Chillán.

A series of events demonstrated the deep enmity and rivalry between Carrera and O'Higgins, and they brought on a civil war among the rebels that weakened them even as the Loyalists' forces were strengthening. In a purely strategic move, O'Higgins and Loyalist troops under General Gabino Gaínza had signed the Treaty of Lircay. This agreement stipulated that the patriots would recognize the Spanish king and that the Spanish would leave the country. The Carrera brothers, meanwhile, had managed to escape their prison in Chillán and travel to Santiago. José Miguel, taking advantage of the discontent occasioned by the Treaty of Lircay, incited the capital's garrison into rebellion and created a junta, placing himself at its head.

O'Higgins refused to recognize Carrera in his new role, and the two generals struggled against one another in a civil war. The viceroy of Peru, unhappy with the Treaty of Lircay, ordered Spanish General Mariano Osorio and a powerful army to march on Santiago from Talcahuano. Before this common danger, Carrera and O'Higgins set aside their differences, with O'Higgins generously accepting Carrera as president of the junta.

Osorio marched on with 5,000 troops; the rebels had an army of 4,000 troops. O'Higgins barricaded himself in Rancagua, some 85 miles south of the capital; Carrera placed himself a short distance to the north, as a rear guard. As O'Higgins awaited the arrival of the Spaniards, he had a black flag placed atop the steeple of the Church of La Merced, indicating that he would not surrender.

Osorio laid siege to the city for two days, cutting of all water supplies and setting fire to the houses. The rebels still resisted. One of Carrera's divisions attempted to come to O'Higgins's assistance but retreated without joining the fighting. Finally, on the afternoon of October 2, 1814, O'Higgins, left with only 300 men out of an original force of 2,000, ordered his men to mount their horses and, placing himself at the forefront, charged out of the square, through the Loyalist forces that had been besieging his troops, and escaped. The disaster at Rancagua put a temporary end to the revolution for independence from Spain. Some of the patriots took refuge in their landholdings, and those who were able to, joined the members of the rebel government and fled across the Andes to the city of Mendoza. The *Patria Vieja* had come to an end; the Spanish colonial government was reestablished and the Reconquest was completed. Three days after the siege of Rancagua, Mariano Osorio entered the capital amid great celebration by the Loyalist crowds.

In reprisal for the rebellion, Osorio abolished the Instituto Nacional and the Public Library, and he exiled the patriot leadership to the island of Juan Fernández. Toward the end of 1815, Osorio was replaced by a new governor, Francisco Casimiro Marcó del Pont. Any semblance of moderation was eliminated. Marcó del Pont governed with extreme violence, establishing a brutal police force known as the Talaveras, under the command of Vicente San Bruno. As a result of the implacable and arbitrary force employed by the reestablished Spanish government, the patriot forces across the Andes in Mendoza began to prepare for the next stage of their revolt against the Spanish Crown.

José de San Martín, born in Yapeyú, Argentina, in 1778, had been educated in Madrid and, like many of his South American compatriots, had fought alongside Spanish rebels struggling to oust French troops from the Iberian Peninsula. In 1812, he had returned to Argentina to fight for the independence of his homeland from Spain. In 1814, San Martín was the governor of the province of Cuyo and was residing in Mendoza. The arrival of Chile's patriots after their defeat across the border solidified for San Martín the idea that in order to seal his own country's independence, he should cross into Chile to liberate it, then continue north to Peru to do likewise there. He collaborated very well with O'Higgins, but since he failed to attract Carrera to his plans, the latter left for Buenos Aires. In the Argentine capital, the rancor between backers of O'Higgins and Carrera grew to such an extreme that the younger Luis Carrera fought a duel against a colonel who had sided with O'Higgins. Near Mendoza, meanwhile, San Martín established his military encampment and prepared for a feat that has come to be compared in scope to Hannibal's crossing of the Alps some 2,000 years earlier.

Among the many protagonists in the struggle for Chilean independence, perhaps no one stands out as much as the colorful Manuel Rodríguez, whom San Martín had met in Mendoza. The Argentine general commissioned him to travel to Chile to spy against the Loyalists and lead mounted insurgencies against the army of Marcó del Pont. Rodríguez was born on February 24, 1786, the son of a minor Spanish civil servant who educated his son in the law. By 1810, the younger Rodríguez had become an enthusiastic proponent of Chilean independence, willingly trading the lawyer's robe for the sword of the guerrilla fighter. He became the model for later rebels against authority, prominent among them the Manuel Rodríguez Patriotic Front, which in the mid-1980s opposed the authoritarianism of General Augusto Pinochet.

The image of Manuel Rodríguez that emerges from the pages of history is that of a man recognized as much for his patriotic zeal as for his roguish character, the latter exhibited in his attempts to further the aims of the rebels against Spain. There was something of both Paul Revere and Robin Hood in Rodríguez that even today elicits the admiration of those who learn about him.

On one occasion, Rodríguez was on a mission from San Martín to visit a friend named Eulogio Celis, who lived in the area of Colchagua, between Curicó and San Fernando, south of Rancagua. As he traveled there, he was seen by a Loyalist patrol and, unable to escape, rapidly continued to his friend's house. As he discussed with Celis a plan to provide provincial guerrillas with weapons, he heard horsemen approaching the residence. At first he felt that surely his time had come, but then he conceived a brilliant idea to deceive the Loyalists. He remembered that his friend Celis had on the premises some stocks that, in his role as a part-time jailer, he used to punish drunkards and minor lawbreakers. Rodríguez quickly assumed the typical expression of a drunkard sleeping off the effects of a night of excessive drinking, and placed his legs in the stocks. The soldiers, upon seeing a man thus imprisoned, asked Celis the reason for his being there. Celis informed them that he was a habitual drunkard who constantly pestered the young women who lived on the hacienda. The officer in charge gave the "drunkard" a few kicks and left with his soldiers after advising Celis not to be excessively harsh with young lovers.

But Manuel Rodríguez's fame rests especially in his ability to disguise himself, whether as a peasant moving freely among the enemy or as a priest entering Loyalist camps to "bless" the Spanish troops who watched over the Andean passes between Chile and Argentina. With small bands he fell upon groups of Spanish troops or raided haciendas owned by those loyal to the Crown.

Rodríguez had publicly expressed a desire to meet Marcó del Pont. On one occasion, disguised as an unkempt peasant, he stood next to the palace doors to await the arrival of the Spanish governor. When the sumptuous carriage appeared at the gate, Rodríguez drew near and opened the coach's golden door, bowing respectfully before Marcó del Pont as the latter descended and disdainfully tossed a coin at the feet of the raggedy peasant. A few hours afterward, all of Santiago was celebrating the daring feat. Marcó del Pont, angry at the effrontery, posted a reward of 1,000 pesos in gold for Rodríguez's capture.

Another time Rodríguez, pursued by a Loyalist picket, took refuge in a church. A few moments after his arrival, the troops rapped at the chapel's doors. A kindly Franciscan admitted them and graciously ushered them in. When the troop leader advised him to turn over the man who had taken asylum inside, the friar told them that there was no one inside as far as he knew, but that he was more than willing to help them search. This he did carefully, covering the entire area down to the smallest corner. The troops finally departed after their unsuccessful search, never realizing that the friar who had so solicitously assisted them had been none other than Manuel Rodríguez.

In January 1817, Rodríguez carried out his last deeds; with some eighty men, he fell on Melipilla, a town halfway between Santiago and San Antonio (on the coast). He and his men took possession of funds that had been gathered through forced contributions, some 1,000 pesos, and, like Robin Hood, distributed the money among the peasants.

On January 21, 1817, after more than two years of preparation, San Martín and O'Higgins left Mendoza, in Argentina, with some 4,000 soldiers. The combined armies crossed the Andes and moved to face Marcó del Pont, the governor of Chile. On February 12, in Chacabuco, Spanish General Rafael Maroto, at the head of the Loyalist army, faced a brilliant cavalry charge led by rebel forces under the command of O'Higgins. He was totally surprised and fell back. San Martín joined O'Higgins's troops in the battle, and by noon of that same day, the patriot victory was complete.

The Spanish defeat at Chacabuco caused many Spaniards, among them Marcó del Pont, to flee the capital. The governor, one of the first to attempt to sail to Peru, was captured along the way and exiled to Argentina, where he died shortly afterward.

The Ejército Libertador (Liberating Army) entered Santiago, where the *cabildo* (town council) offered San Martín the position of dictator of Chile, an offer that he refused. The assembly then named O'Higgins supreme director of Chile. With the battle of Chacabuco, the Reconquest ended and the *Patria Nueva* (New Fatherland) began. Another year would pass, however, before Chile truly achieved independence.

After the defeat at Chacabuco, the remnants of Spain's army, under the command of Captain José Ordóñez, had taken refuge in Concepción. O'Higgins sent Colonel Juan Gregorio de Las Heras to dislodge these forces. Las Heras defeated Ordóñez and the Loyalist troops retreated, taking refuge in Talcahuano, a port just north of Concepción. The Chileans laid siege unsuccessfully to Talcahuano, losing 600 men in the process. O'Higgins traveled south and laid siege to the city for four and a half months; he attacked it in December 1817, again without managing to dislodge the Loyalist troops.

In January 1818, Joaquín de la Pezuela, viceroy of Peru, sent a second expeditionary force to Chile. These troops, under the command of General Mariano Osorio, the victor at Rancagua, landed in Talcahuano; O'Higgins lifted his siege of the city and traveled north. He stopped in Talca, and he made the decision to test the sentiments of the nation's citizens. In every city, two books were opened for a vote, for or against independence. Those in favor of independence were filled; those against, were left blank. With the assurance he had been given by this vote, O'Higgins signed the Declaration of Independence. On February 12, 1818, exactly one year after Chacabuco, the authorities throughout the nation affirmed the independence of Chile.

After several additional battles between rebel and Loyalist forces, Bernardo O'Higgins, wounded in the arm in a previous skirmish, and José de San Martín, came together and faced Mariano Osorio at Maipo, some 25 miles from the center of Santiago, for the decisive battle of the war. It was April 5, 1818. The battle turned in favor of the Chileans and Osorio retreated toward Talcahuano, where he boarded a ship and escaped to Lima. By mid-1818, Chile was free of Spanish control from Copiapó to Concepción. The *Patria Nueva* had ended; the Chilean Republic had begun.

Modern-day Chilean historians have examined the realities of the revolutionary war that led to the separation of Chile from Spain. The rose-colored glasses through which nostalgic minds have historically viewed the period between 1808 and 1818, and beyond, are beginning to be discarded in favor of a more clear-eyed and impartial study of the complexities of the period.

O'Higgins, greatly influenced by the ideas of Francisco de Miranda, the Venezuelan proponent of Latin American independence, had returned to Chile from a long residence in England and the Continent as one of a small but committed minority of *criollos* who espoused the cause of independence from Spain. He had joined a secret revolutionary group known as the Logia Lautarina, in honor of the legendary Lautaro, whose goal was the promotion of Spanish American independence. Membership was secret; its adherents were expected to submit for prior approval the names of all those they would nominate for military, government, and official positions. The lodge's critics saw it as a group of anticlerical, Masonic subversives dedicated to the destruction of the old order, something which, of course, was not far from the truth.

The Years After 1818

After the eight years of revolution (1810–1818), O'Higgins, as supreme director, moved toward the establishment of the republic. Under his leadership, public works were undertaken, among them the reopening of the National Institute and the Public Library. He founded the Military Academy, today known as the Bernardo O'Higgins Military School, and the Cementerio General (General Cemetery), the largest in the nation. He created the

Legion of Merit, an award to be bestowed on those who distinguished themselves through service to the nation. Santiago's main thoroughfare, the Alameda de las Delicias, today officially known as Avenida Bernardo O'Higgins,
was created under his leadership. That avenue, which runs almost the entire
breadth of the city from east to west before changing name and leading to
the foot of the Andes, bisects the city, and since the mid-1970s marks the
path of the main subway line. Most *santiaguinos* combine the two names
when they refer to the thoroughfare as "Alameda Bernardo O'Higgins."

During the first months of independence, O'Higgins saw the necessity to
create a national navy to protect the security of Chile, a nation that, clearly,
depended very heavily upon its many miles of Pacific coast, a dependence
that was to grow significantly throughout the rest of the nineteenth century.
Although Chile's independence had been realized after Maipo, the Loyalists
still occupied the southern part of the country and controlled the sea.
O'Higgins acquired four ships—the *Lautaro*, the *Chacabuco*, the *Araucano*,
and the *San Martín*—from England and the United States. To these he added
the brigantine *Aguila*, captured in Valparaíso from the Spaniards after the
victory at Chacabuco. These five ships became the nucleus of the First Naval
Squadron, placed under the command of Blanco Encalada, an Argentine
colonel who had served in the Spanish navy. The first naval feat of the young
squadron was the capture of the Spanish frigate *María Isabel*, toward the end
of 1818; it had been sent to Talcahuano with Spanish troops to reinforce
the forces in the area. This ship, christened the *O'Higgins*, became the sixth
member of the fleet.

At about the same time, the distinguished British sailor Lord Thomas
Cochrane arrived in Chile and offered his services to the new nation. He was
the first of many such adventurers and immigrants who were to cement
lasting ties between Chile and the British Isles. O'Higgins gave him command of the fleet with the title of vice admiral. The new vice admiral made
two trips along the coast of Peru in search of Spanish ships, but they had
taken refuge inside that country's port of Callao. Lord Cochrane then
planned the capture of the city of Valdivia, which was still under the control
of the Spanish. In February 1820, in a daring amphibian assault, Cochrane,
with 300 men, attacked and captured the city's plaza, defended by nearly
1,000 Spaniards.

Cochrane returned to Valparaíso in glory, and accepted the command of
the fleet that was to take José de San Martín, head of the expedition, on his
voyage to liberate Peru. On August 1820, the Liberation Squadron left Valparaíso and sailed north toward Peru. The Army of Liberation, under the

command of San Martín, disembarked at Pisco, some 130 miles south of Lima, and set up camp there. The fleet, under Cochrane, sailed north to blockade Callao. During the night of November 5, 1820, Cochrane and his men quietly approached the Spanish ship *Esmeralda* in small boats, under the cover of darkness. Cochrane was the first to board the ship and, after sustained, hand-to-hand fighting, took control of the vessel. The *Esmeralda*, now the newest ship in the Chilean navy, was to play a historic role in the War of the Pacific, almost six decades later.

The impetuous Lord Cochrane and San Martín had serious disagreements; as a result, the British adventurer left Peru and later moved to Brazil. San Martín entered Lima, having fought no significant battles, and proclaimed the independence of Peru on July 28, 1821. The new nation bestowed on him the title Protector of Peru.

The joint Argentine-Chilean expeditionary force did not achieve its projected goals. At a famous private and mysterious meeting between San Martín and Venezuelan liberator Simón Bolívar, in the Ecuadoran city of Guayaquil, the future of the continent was decided. For reasons never completely understood or explained, San Martín relinquished his position as coleader, ceding command to Bolívar, and returned to Chile. Shortly afterward, he crossed over to Argentina, and finally chose self-exile in Europe, where he died in 1850.

Chile also had its own Benedict Arnold, in the person of Vicente Benavides, a Chilean who twice betrayed his country. He began as a patriot, then went over to the Spanish side. He was taken prisoner at Maipo and was sentenced to die by firing squad. Amazingly, the bullets fired at him only scratched his skin. Benavides feigned death, and later escaped. He spent seven months in hiding until, one day, he appeared before San Martín and managed to convince the general to pardon him. He rejoined the patriot army only to desert again, this time stating publicly that he was an implacable enemy of the patriot cause. He carried out pillaging raids from Chillán southward, accompanied by the Pincheira brothers, who, under the pretext of being supporters of Spanish sovereignty, assaulted and robbed as they pleased. Benavides was sought by national leaders including Ramón Freire, Manuel Bulnes, and Joaquín Prieto, all of whom later served as president of the nation. He finally was caught while trying to escape to Peru aboard a launch, and was hanged in Santiago in 1822.

Several of O'Higgins's government directives led to rising opposition from the ranks of those who stood to suffer most from them. The establishment of Protestant cemeteries and the introduction of Protestant teachers to develop an anticlerical educational system, among other measures, weakened O'Higgins's position in the new republic. Certain aristocrats, fearful of losing privileges, resented the elimination of titles of nobility.

While San Martín and O'Higgins had been organizing the Army of the Andes in Mendoza, the Carrera brothers stayed in Buenos Aires. Miguel Carrera, not wanting to remain inactive and uninvolved in the struggle against the Loyalists, sailed to the United States to seek support for his own efforts back in Chile. After one year he managed to obtain five ships and arms on credit. He also gathered a select group of French and English officers with whom he returned to Buenos Aires, in 1817, planning to continue on to the Pacific. However, Martín de Pueyrredón, supreme director of Argentina, put Carrera in prison and took possession of his ships. Carrera managed to escape and fled to Montevideo.

Meanwhile, Miguel's brothers, Juan José and Luis, left Buenos Aires secretly and traveled incognito towards Chile, since the Argentine government was impeding such movement. They were traveling separately, but since their movements had been closely watched, they were captured and reunited in Mendoza, where they were jailed. Their political enemies could find no evidence against them, so they arranged for them to "escape" with the assistance of supposed supporters. Juan José and Luis fell for the deceit and attempted to flee. Charged with attempted escape, they were sentenced to death and were executed by firing squad in the public square of Mendoza on April 8, 1818.

In Montevideo, José Miguel received the news of the execution and swore to avenge the deaths of his brothers. He returned to Argentina, and there joined with the federal caudillos (leaders) who opposed the unitarian government in Buenos Aires. For two years he fought alongside these forces as they struggled to overthrow the central government. His fame as a successful guerrilla spread rapidly during this time, and as he was planning to cross the Andes to Chile, he was betrayed by his Argentine allies and turned over to the governor of Mendoza. After a brief court-martial he was condemned to death.

On September 4, 1821, exactly ten years to the day since he had commenced his public life in Santiago, Miguel Carrera was led to the place of execution—the same spot where, three years earlier, his brothers had been shot.

The executioner approached Miguel Carrera in order to place a blindfold over his eyes, but the condemned man indignantly refused this customary gesture. He requested that, instead of being seated on the prisoner's dock, he be allowed to die on his feet, with his eyes uncovered. He also asked that he himself be permitted to give the order to fire.

The officer in charge acceded to the first two of these requests but let Carrera know that it was not in his purview to allow the third. The prisoner placed his right hand over his heart to indicate the place where the firing squad should aim. Two bullets hit him in the heart and two went through his forehead. At the age of thirty-five, José Miguel Carrera was dead. In 1828 his remains, along with those of his brothers, were taken to Chile. In 1864 the public raised the funds to erect a statue in honor of Miguel. That monument stands on Santiago's central artery, the Alameda Bernardo O'Higgins.

Another patriot who proved to be a political thorn in O'Higgins's side was the popular Manuel Rodríguez, a friend of the Carreras. Aware of his popularity with the public, O'Higgins unsuccessfully tried to distance him from the nation by offering him a diplomatic post in the United States. San Martín, himself an admirer of Rodríguez, also was unable to pacify the restless master of disguise.

One day, Manuel Rodríguez daringly entered the yard of the governmental palace, riding a horse and leading a tumultuous throng of citizens. O'Higgins ordered that he be imprisoned at the barracks of the Los Andes chasseurs (rapid movement troops), and a legal process was instituted against him. Shortly afterward, the chasseurs were ordered transferred to Quillota, close to 80 miles northwest of Santiago. The regiment started out from the capital, taking their illustrious prisoner with them. On May 26, 1818, Antonio Navarro, the officer in charge of guarding him, intimated to Rodríguez that he might be able to escape with his compliance, and invited the prisoner to slip away from the troops. Out of sight of the regiment, Navarro shot Rodríguez in the back, mortally wounding him. He was later to claim that the prisoner had been attempting to escape. Rodríguez's remains were later transferred to Santiago and now rest in the Cementerio General. There is an equestrian statue of him on the Avenida General Bustamante in Santiago.

Great mystery surrounds the Logia Lautarina, whose prime purpose was to support and serve the cause of Chilean independence. So secretive was the organization that its membership was never known in its entirety, even though it remained active until 1822. It has been believed that the deaths of the Carreras and Manuel Rodríguez were authorized by the Logia, especially given the prominent place occupied by O'Higgins within its membership.

It is indisputable that O'Higgins's government was a dictatorship. His stated belief was that, all other means failing, force would be the only approach to carry out what was, in his view, best for the young nation. Upon rising to power, he dictated the provisional constitution of 1818. He was under pressure to create a legislative senate and a political constitution but he resisted, feeling that the nation was unprepared for them. Finally, in 1822, he approved a new constitution that was promulgated without the participation or input of the citizenry. It bestowed on O'Higgins almost all of the powers given him in the earlier provisional document and extended his mandate. The mayor of Concepción, Ramón Freire, rose up against O'Higgins and marched on Santiago at the head of his troops.

In the capital, the most influential citizens gathered at the Consulate on January 28, 1823. They called on O'Higgins to appear before them so that he would be present during their deliberations. Their consensus was that the supreme director should step down from power to avoid the disturbances that would materialize as Freire and his troops neared the city and support for his dictatorship waned. O'Higgins informed those present that he would not recognize their authority to ask that he abandon power, but, faced with the obviously inevitable loss of support, he proposed the creation of a provisional junta to which he could relinquish his command. Once such a body had been accepted and created, O'Higgins surrendered the presidential sash, signed his papers of abdication, and left. He was acclaimed for the apparent magnanimity of this act even by those who had opposed him. Days later, he boarded a ship in Valparaíso, and sailed to Peru in voluntary exile. In Lima, O'Higgins was given the Montalván hacienda, where he lived with his mother, Isabel Riquelme; his half-sister, Rosa Rodríguez; and his out-of-wedlock son, Demetrio. He always planned to return to his native land, but he died on October 24, 1842, before this hope became a reality. His remains were repatriated in 1869 and he is buried in the Cementerio General in Santiago.

There are several monuments to Chile's national hero; the most imposing and recognized is an equestrian statue on the boulevard named for him, the Avenida Libertador Bernardo O'Higgins, also known as the Alameda. It depicts the general exhorting his soldiers as they prepare to charge out of the siege of Rancagua. Across from this monument and facing the statue of O'Higgins is an equally majestic memorial to the other great figure of Chilean independence, José de San Martín. Both equestrian statues stand in front of La Moneda, the nation's government palace.

The period from O'Higgins's abdication in 1823 until 1830 was one of political uncertainty and unrest. There was a succession of ideologies, personalities, presidents, and political rebellions. Ramón Freire, who had led the revolt against O'Higgins from Concepción, governed the country from 1823 until 1826, returning to office briefly in 1827, and even attempting an invasion of Chile from Peru in 1836. The period from 1823 through 1829 was associated with several attempts to mold Chile into either liberalism or federalism, in part mirroring similar experiments across the Andes in Argentina. Exponents of European liberalism tried to effect changes in Chile's traditional administrative, economic, and social structure. The implementation of these liberal principles led to direct conflict with Chile's most conservative social institution, the Catholic Church. O'Higgins, Freire, and other political leaders had been anticlerical and had preached religious toleration. Some prominent *criollo* families resisted the attempts at liberalization most bitterly.

Influential intellectuals who admired the federalist example in the United States proposed creating such a system in Chile, so as to promote regional autonomy and decentralization, and effect a loosening of the political domination emanating from Santiago and Valparaíso. Both liberalism and federalism, however, proved to be inconsistent with the reality of Hispanic capitalism that Chile had inherited from Spain, but this did not prevent experimentation with both of them during these years of anarchy and factionalism.

Two political parties struggled for power and political direction. On one side were the conservatives, known in Chile as the *pelucones* (bigwigs), defenders of traditional principles, among them the privileges of the Church. The other faction, known as the *pipiolos* (upstarts or novices), supported liberal or federalist principles. Anarchy ruled, however, for factions developed within these two parties. Consequently, there followed a period marked by a quick succession of presidents and constitutions, accompanied by opposing armies supporting one faction or another. At the same time, bandits roamed the countryside almost unchecked.

The political uncertainty that prevailed in Chile was mirrored throughout the rest of the former Spanish colonies. An alliance composed of Austria, Prussia, and Russia, the so-called Holy Alliance, conspired to support Spain and its monarch, Ferdinand VII, in an attempt to recover its dominion over the nations, from Mexico to Argentina, which had recently achieved their political separation from the mother country.

In 1824, the government of the United States was faced with the potential return of former colonial powers to the newly emancipated colonies to the south. With equal measures of self-interest and altruism, President James Monroe issued his well-known proclamation that the American continent was no longer open to colonization by the European powers. The Monroe

Doctrine, although proclaimed by a young and relatively weak nation, served at least partially to stem the ambition of the Holy Alliance to effect a return to the American continent.

These conditions of political uncertainty produced a concurrent instability in the economy. Tax evasion, brought about in large measure by the ever-shifting government authorities, was widespread, with farmers keeping back up to 40 percent of the taxes levied upon them. Corruption in the administration and in the customhouse also kept needed revenue from the government treasury. The peasantry, assessed a *diezmo* (tithe), also tended to evade such taxes either out of inability to pay them or from the desire to keep back a substantial portion of it. Tax enforcement tended to be halfhearted and inconsistent due to the instability of the authorities.

Finally, the political and economic chaos that reigned during this second decade of the nineteenth century brought about an alliance of businessmen and military leaders who would ultimately succeed in making Chile an oasis of stability in a continent fraught with revolution and economic mismanagement.

Diego Portales

The central figure who brought about this stabilization was Diego Portales, a businessman born in Santiago in 1793, the son of an influential royal officer who had served as superintendent of the mint. An aristocrat of Basque-Castilian ancestry, Portales exhibited an extreme distaste for liberalism, and he consequently allied himself with conservative interests, the leadership of the Church, and military patriots who thought as he did, among them Joaquín Prieto, president of Chile for two consecutive five-year terms (1831–1841), and Manuel Bulnes, who succeeded Prieto in the presidency (1841–1851). Portales's solution for the instability that followed the wars of independence was a return to fiscal integrity, law and order, and the restoration of the legitimacy that he felt had existed before the liberal policies of many of the heroes of the independence movement.

Portales first showed great political skills under the brief presidency of José Joaquín Ovalle (1830–1831), who appointed him to two cabinet posts, minister of the interior and minister of war. Under President Prieto, Portales became chief minister and informal adviser; he was offered the office of vice president but refused it. He was instrumental in suffocating the *pipiolos* and containing all revolutionary attempts that might upset the conservative policies of the governments which had consolidated the political stability that Chile was now beginning to exhibit. Portales, a symbol of conservative in-

This statue of Chile's most famous secretary of state, Diego Portales, is on the Plaza de la Constitución (Constitution Square) in Santiago, facing the presidential palace, La Moneda.

flexibility, had little use for constitutions or formal principles; he was a pragmatic leader who rejected any legalities that might return the nation to the instability which had been finally laid aside. Chile elaborated a new constitution in 1833, a document that was to serve as the legal foundation for the country until 1891. Although Portales contributed little to its drafting, the 1833 constitution became known as the document that institutionalized what has come to be known as the Portalian state.

Portales favored the institutionalization of a strong, central government that would stabilize the nation politically and economically. A benevolent despot, he rejected representative democracy, popular suffrage, and liberalism. The Constitution of 1833 formalized many of the principles espoused by Portales and by his coreligionist Mariano Egaña, the document's principal author. It provided for a strong executive who had the authority to declare a state of siege when he deemed it necessary and when Congress was not in session. Such a declaration entitled the president to suspend all constitutional guarantees in the affected territory. The executive was also empowered to appoint governors and intendants who would, thus, be able to function as his direct agents and allies. Still, the Congress was empowered to approve the annual budget, levy taxes, and control the size of the military. The inevitable conflicts that were engendered by two such strong branches of government led, finally, to a head-on collision between the legislative and executive branches in the civil war of 1891.

The 1833 Constitution also maintained Roman Catholicism as the state religion and banned the public exercise of all other faiths. Freedom of religious expression, which had been supported by many of those who fought the war of independence, among them O'Higgins, was restricted. Not until 1925 was there a formal separation of Church and state.

The right to vote was restricted to those who were deemed to be qualified by income or literacy. Because of lax enforcement of the literacy requirement, wealthy landowners were often able to enroll their tenant farmers in the voting rolls and manipulate them to support the candidates who would maintain the status quo. Military commanders did likewise with their troops, maneuvering them to vote along the same lines. The alliance between landowners, merchants, the Church, and the military, which had succeeded in restoring law and order, ensured that Chile would largely avoid the instability that characterized much of the rest of Latin America for the rest of the nineteenth century and a good part of the twentieth. As has been noted by many political experts, new constitutions do not, of themselves, guarantee political stability, especially in Latin America. Several events, all of them essentially fortuitous, helped to cement the unique stability that Chile had begun to enjoy with the political arrival of Portales, which continued for several decades and generally into the next century.

Ramón Freire, successor to Bernardo O'Higgins and twice president (1823–1826 and 1827), had been exiled to Peru but in 1830 attempted a return to power in Chile, gathering troops and armaments with which he planned to overthrow the government of Francisco Prieto (1827–1829). His plot failed and he was again exiled, this time to Australia, from which, in 1836, he returned to Chile but remained removed from politics. Relations between Chile and Peru had been tense because Freire's attempt had originated in Lima, and also because Peru had failed to repay the loan extended to San Martín to cover the cost of his expeditionary force to liberate Peru from Spain.

In 1825, Bolivia, originally a part of the Viceroyalty of Peru, became an independent state and was governed for a short time by Bolívar, in whose honor the new nation was named. When Bolívar gave up his leadership, the country's Asamblea (Assembly) elected Antonio José de Sucre, Bolívar's second in command, president of the nation (1825–1828). Not long after, a revolution forced Sucre to abandon his position and Marshal Andrés de Santa Cruz governed from 1829 until 1839.

In 1836, Santa Cruz, taking advantage of the rivalry that existed between two Peruvian caudillos, Luis José de Orbegoso (president of the nation 1833–1835) and Felipe S. Salaverry (president 1835–1836), invaded Peru, with the support of Orbegoso; overthrew President Agustín Gamarra; unified Peru and Bolivia as the Peru-Bolivia Confederation; and assumed power, taking the title of Protector.

Portales saw the Confederation as a threat to Chilean interests. A series of political and diplomatic events solidified Chilean opposition to the union of its two neighbors. The Chilean Congress declared war on the new state, making several demands on Santa Cruz: indemnification for the Freire expedition, satisfaction for injuries and slights suffered by Chilean diplomats while in Peru, repayment of the loan extended for the San Martín expedition of liberation years earlier, dissolution of the Confederation, and a limit on Peru's naval forces. When Santa Cruz rejected the demands, Prieto's government declared a state of siege throughout Chile, bestowing emergency dictatorial powers on Portales.

In June 1837, mutinous troops led by Colonel José Antonio Vidaurre assassinated Portales. The government defeated these troops, and Vidaurre and other conspirators were later apprehended and executed for their part in the assassination. Portales became a Chilean martyr, and the government tried to link his death to actions carried out by agents of Santa Cruz in Chile.

The death of Portales did not upset or thwart Chile's plans against the Peru-Bolivia Confederation. Admiral Manuel Blanco Encalada was sent to Peru with 2,700 men to do battle with the armies of Santa Cruz. Faced by superior forces and imminent defeat, Encalada recognized the Confederation and signed the Pact of Paucarpata, returning to Chile in November 1837.

The Chilean government rejected the outcome of this first expeditionary force and, months later, prepared and sent a second army under the command of General Manuel Bulnes. The Chilean leader disembarked near Lima with a vastly superior force of 6,000 men and defeated Santa Cruz at two different sites while an English ally, Robert Simpson, who had served under Lord Cochrane, repulsed the Confederation's naval forces. Finally, the Chi-

leans under Bulnes convincingly defeated the bulk of Santa Cruz's army at
the Battle of Yungay, in 1839, and effectively dissolved the Peru-Bolivia
Confederation. Bulnes returned to Chile a hero and succeeded Joaquín Prieto
as president, serving from 1841 to 1851.

During his presidency, Bulnes collaborated with the hard-working minister of education, Manuel Montt, later president in his own right, in pro-
moting public education. The University of Chile was founded in Santiago
in 1842, succeeding the colonial University of San Felipe, which had ceased
to exist in 1839. Its first rector was the Venezuelan Andrés Bello, a man
whose influence on Chilean education and culture were incalculable. Having
been invited by many of the new nations of Spanish America to take up
residence and share his considerable talents in the promotion and creation
of national institutions, Bello chose Chile and settled there, remaining for
forty years, until his death in 1865.

The Normal School for Teachers was inaugurated on June 14, 1842, the
first of its kind in Spanish America and chronologically second only to the
oldest in the United States, which opened two years earlier. Its first director
was the renowned Argentine writer and educator (and, later, president of
that nation) Domingo Faustino Sarmiento, who lived for many years in
Chile. The National Conservatory of Music and the Academy of Painting
were further additions to the cultural enrichment of the nation. The first
Normal School for Women was founded in 1853.

Sarmiento and Bello were not alone in sharing their considerable talents
with Chile. Many other foreigners either settled in Chile during this early
period of the nation's independence or contributed significantly to the development of its national institutions and infrastructure.

Prominent among them was William Wheelwright, an American industrialist who introduced steam navigation and the railroad to the nation. Up-
permost in his mind was the creation of a steamship line that would serve
the nation's interests along the Pacific. To bring his project to fruition,
Wheelwright traveled to London; he returned to his new country with two
ships, aptly named the *Chile* and the *Peru*. The two vessels were warmly
received in Valparaíso in 1840 and formed the vanguard of the new steamship
service between that port and Panama.

Although his creation of this first steam line between Chile's major port
and Panama was a significant achievement for him and for Chile, Wheelwright's major contribution to the nation was the construction of the nation's
and South America's first railroad, which connected the two important mining centers of Caldera and Copiapó. The service was inaugurated on July 4,
1851, and its first locomotive is displayed today in Copiapó at the Mining

School. Wheelwright also proposed a railroad between Santiago and Valparaíso, to be built by another North American industrialist, Henry Meiggs. Service between Chile's two main cities was in existence by 1863 and was later extended to San Fernando, south of the capital.

Wheelwright's contributions extended beyond the construction of the first railroad. Under his direction, the first telegraph line was erected to serve Santiago and Valparaíso in the period 1851–1852. A quarter of a century later, service connected some forty-eight Chilean cities and provided connections to Peru and Argentina. The creation of transportation and communication links helped the nation to enjoy a boom in commerce between 1845 and 1875; the number of ships entering and leaving the port of Valparaíso more than doubled in the decade between 1860 and 1870.

Chile's ethnic crucible also included eminent individuals from several European nations. José Joaquín de Mora, Spanish writer and educator, founded the Liceo de Chile (Public School) in 1827. Another Spaniard, the physician Manuel Julián Grajales, introduced vaccination to the nation in 1807, and his compatriot, Andrés Antonio Gorbea, a renowned mathematician, founded the first engineering school. Lorenzo Sazie, a French physician, directed the College of Medicine. Ignacio Domeyko, Polish geologist and mineralogist, promoted scientific principles in the mining industry.

After an initial period of political and economic turbulence, Chile had finally established normalcy and continuity in its efforts to solidify its independence, its nascent national institutions, and its unique place among the new nations of Spanish America. The Portalian state, not democratic from the perspective afforded by contemporary realities, did allow Chile to direct its energies in directions that most of its Hispanic neighbors continued to be unable to follow due to political and economic instability.

The Bulnes presidency ended in 1851. Manuel Montt, his successor, governed until 1861. During his presidency, the government promulgated the Civil Code, under the direction of Andrés Bello. Montt further expanded public instruction, founding a normal school, an institution to educate the deaf and the mute, and the Casa de Orates, to house the mentally ill. To promote economic expansion, he created the Caja de Crédito Hipotecario, with the intention of making funds available to those needing mortgages.

Also during Montt's presidency, the immigration of German colonists to settle and develop the large area of Chile south of the national capital was promoted. Today, cities such as Valdivia and Llanquihue, Puerto Varas and Puerto Montt bear the clear mark of the considerable influence of these industrious colonists. Puerto Varas was named in honor of Montt's minister of the interior.

José Joaquín Pérez (1861–1871) was the last to serve as president for two consecutive five-year terms. An amendment to the Constitution, enacted in 1871, prohibited the immediate reelection of a president once his five-year term of office had been served. In 1866, a war broke out between Chile and Spain when the former went to the aid of Peru, whose Chincha Islands had been occupied and appropriated by Spain. Brief skirmishes resulted in Spain's bombardment of Valparaíso and Chile's taking of the Spanish ship *Covadonga*, a vessel which would play a significant role in the War of the Pacific, which pitted Chile against Bolivia and Peru.

Federico Errázuriz Zañartu, elected president in 1871, was the first to serve only one five-year term, in accordance with the constitutional amendment of 1871. He was the first president to be a member of the Liberal party and, as such, broke the trend established under Portales back in the 1830s. A very active administrator, Errázuriz was instrumental in extending the railroad to the southern city of Angol, some 600 kilometers (375 miles) south of Santiago. Architectural achievements included the construction of the National University and the Palacio del Congreso (Congress Building). The Penal Code was approved and the navy's strength was augmented by the addition of two ships, the *Blanco* and the *Cochrane*. Although elected with the support of the Conservatives, Errázuriz governed with the support of the Liberals and Radicals beginning in 1873. This fusion, called the Alianza Liberal (Liberal Alliance), effectively led to theological battles instigated by the government's renewed promotion of liberal ideas, among them the suppression of the ecclesiastical privileges enjoyed by the Church. Like O'Higgins and other liberals during the early years of independence, Errázuriz advocated the creation of nonreligious cemeteries, civil marriage and registration, and the separation of Church and state. These changes were not accepted and carried out until the early years of the next century.

The War of the Pacific (1879–1884)

Aníbal Pinto (1876–1881) served as president during one of Chile's most significant events, the War of the Pacific, fought against Peru and Bolivia. That international event created a serious economic and political crisis, and another conflict also preoccupied Pinto's administration: the question of stable and final settlement of Chile's borders with Argentina. That conflict was to bring the two countries close to war more than once during the twentieth century, and would occasion differences well into the late 1990s. The first border conflict with Argentina was settled in 1881, when Chile and Argentina agreed that the border between them would be established by a line passing along the highest peaks of the Andes. As a result, Chile was left in possession of the Strait of Magellan and Argentina would have sovereignty over eastern Patagonia.

The War of the Pacific marked the three nations involved in ways that no event had before, even the wars of independence from Spain in the period between 1810 and 1825. Today, Chile continues to enjoy the fruits of its victory even as Peru, and especially Bolivia, suffer the consequences of their defeat. Chile's national territory, economic wealth, military preeminence, and national pride all grew significantly. Although both Peru and Bolivia lost territory as a result of Chile's definitive victory, it was the second and poorer of the two, Bolivia, which suffered most; it lost considerably more land area than Peru, and its access to the Pacific as well, as Chile increased its national sovereignty to north of the 19th parallel, to the city of Arica and, for a few decades, as far as Tacna (today again a part of Peru). Chile's territorial gains could be compared to those experienced by the United States after either the Louisiana Purchase of 1803 or the Mexican–American War that ended in 1848. The important cities of Iquique and Antofagasta, situated in areas rich in nitrate and copper, became part of Chile's national territory. Chile became the most important producer of saltpeter, an important element in the production of gunpowder and fertilizer; deposits within its borders account for more than 95 percent of the world's reserves. The income derived from the exploitation and exportation of this natural resource made Chile a comparatively wealthy nation. The Germans' discovery of a process to extract nitrogen from the air, during World War I, put an end to Chile's domination of the world's nitrate market, although this resource continues to play an important, albeit a lesser, role in the nation's income.

The conflict began in February 1879, when Chile occupied the port city of Antofagasta in an attempt to prevent the Bolivian government from auctioning off the nitrate fields, then in the hands of the Compañía Chilena de Salitre de Antofagasta (Chilean Nitrate Company of Antofagasta). The company had refused to pay what it considered outrageous tariffs imposed on it by Bolivia, and the latter had employed that refusal to put its 1866 and 1874 treaties with Chile in a vulnerable position. When Chile's troops occupied Antofagasta, the president of Bolivia, Hilarión Daza, declared war on Chile, purportedly with the secret support of Peru, then governed by General Mariano Prado. Chile, in possession of documents that exposed a secret alliance between its two northern neighbors that dated back to 1873, declared war on both of them on April 5, 1879. The War of the Pacific was on.

Chile's undisputed military hero of the war, to many on an equal footing with Bernardo O'Higgins, is Arturo Prat Chacón (1848–1879), who gained his place in the pantheon of heroes at the naval battle of Iquique, the most heroic and, at the same time, gentlemanly romantic battle of the war.

It was dawn, May 21, 1879, and the port of Iquique, then Peruvian, was being blockaded by two Chilean naval vessels, the *Esmeralda* and the *Covadonga*. Carlos Condell was the second ship's captain; the *Esmeralda* was under the command of Prat, a thirty-one-year-old naval officer who had distinguished himself in the brief war against Spain in 1866. Both the *Esmeralda* and the *Covadonga* were old wooden ships, anomalies in a naval world rapidly converting to metal, armored ships of the type that Peru would bring to bear that morning.

When the *Covadonga*'s guardsman made out smoke in the distance, both ships prepared themselves for combat. Two Peruvian armored battleships, the *Huáscar*, named in honor of the half brother of Atahualpa, the last Inca emperor, and the *Independencia*, were rapidly approaching the two Chilean vessels that were blockading the port city. Prat, realizing that the *Esmeralda* and the *Covadonga* would be unable to withstand an attack by the vastly superior Peruvian ships, said the following words, later to be inscribed in Chile's history books and taught to children in school:

"Lads! The battle is unevenly matched. Never has our flag been lowered before the enemy, and I hope that this will not be the time when it is done. As long as I live, that flag will wave in its place; if I die, my officers will know where their duty lies."

The *Esmeralda* withstood fire from the port's batteries as well as from the *Huáscar*'s guns for more than two hours. Finally, the Peruvian captain, Miguel Grau, decided to put an end to the battle, and he gave the command to crush the *Esmeralda* with the *Huáscar*'s battering ram. As Grau's ship battered the *Esmeralda* with its ram the first time, Prat, sword in hand, beckoned his men to jump aboard the *Huáscar* and fight on the enemy ship. Shouting, "¡Al abordaje!" (Follow me aboard!), Prat and those of his men who were able to hear him in the clamor of the battle, jumped onto the *Huáscar*'s deck, where they were quickly cut down by a fusillade of bullets.

The *Huáscar* pulled away from the *Esmeralda* and then proceeded to ram it again. After this second blow, another officer and twelve of his men jumped aboard the *Huáscar* as Prat had done; they suffered the same fate. The Peruvian ship discharged its cannon several more times and rammed the *Esmeralda* a third time. The Chilean ship slowly began to sink as Ernesto Riquelme, the last surviving midshipman, fired one last salvo and went down with the ship. Of the 180 men who had been aboard the *Esmeralda*, 60 survived, all of them picked up by boats from the *Huáscar*.

Aboard the *Covadonga*, Condell decided to even the field of battle by inducing the *Independencia* to give chase to his smaller and weaker ship. Since Condell knew that the Peruvian ship had a deeper keel, he sailed close to the coast and caused the *Independencia* to run aground. His ship proceeded to turn its guns on the more powerful ship in hopes of forcing the Peruvian captain to surrender. The *Huáscar*, however, now victorious over the *Esmeralda*, came to the rescue of the *Independencia*, and the *Covadonga* fled toward Antofagasta. For five months after the naval battle of Iquique, the *Huáscar* adroitly avoided a head-on meeting with the Chilean fleet. Then, in an event reminiscent of the World War II struggle between the British Navy and the German battleship *Bismarck*, two Chilean ships, the *Cochrane* and the *Blanco*, surprised the *Huáscar* at Mejillones, just north of Antofagasta, and forced it to do battle. Accurate and fortuitous shots from the *Cochrane* hit the *Huáscar*'s bridge and killed its captain, Miguel Grau. After two other commanders aboard the Peruvian monitor were also killed, the survivors aboard the *Huáscar* surrendered to the Chileans. With the *Huáscar*'s capture, Chile obtained complete supremacy in the Pacific.

After the sinking of the *Esmeralda*, Grau, in a chivalric gesture typical of nineteenth-century wars, supervised the transfer of the remains of Prat and his men for burial in Iquique. He safeguarded Prat's briefcase, along with his photographs of his wife and children, and his sword. Later, Grau sent the briefcase and sword to Prat's widow, along with a letter of condolence praising his vanquished enemy. After his own death, Grau's remains were transported to Santiago and given a hero's burial there. (Today, Grau's remains are interred in Lima, in an imposing mausoleum of that city's main cemetery.)

At present, the *Huáscar* is a floating museum anchored in the Chilean port of Talcahuano, just a few miles north of Concepción. On board, visitors can appreciate both the relative might of the monitor and its smallness. Several spots on the deck show where each of the Chilean participants of the Battle of Iquique fought and died. The headquarters where Grau lost his life months later is also marked. Inside the ship, in Grau's quarters, the correspondence between Grau and Prat's widow, as well as the weapons that each participant had wielded, are on display.

Arturo Prat's remains were transferred to Valparaíso in 1888 and interred inside a crypt under a monument that commemorates the heroes of the Battle of Iquique.

The war on land and on the sea continued from 1879 to 1881. Chile's original border with Bolivia had originally been set at the 23rd parallel, just north of the port of Taltal, at Paposo, some 350 kilometers (220 miles) south of the city of Antofagasta, at that time Bolivian territory. Bolivia's border with Peru was set farther north, along a line that marked the border between the provinces of Antofagasta and Tarapacá, halfway between the 21st and the 22nd parallels. Until the war's beginning, the three belligerents had maintained relatively small armies, untrained and ill-prepared to fight a modern war.

However, Chile's army, which in 1879 had numbered only some 2,500 men, had grown to 45,000 by the end of the war. Peru and Bolivia's armies, although they outnumbered their foe's, had suffered from the effects of half a century of political strife and disorganization. After the capture of the *Huáscar*, late in 1879, Chile controlled the sea. The capture of Pisagua and Iquique by Chile's forces caused internal dissension in the governments of Bolivia and Peru, and both of their presidents were ousted as a result. Early in 1880, Chile entered Arica and Tacna, both in Peruvian territory. A bloody battle followed, with casualties reaching more than 5,000. By May 1880, Chile had taken control of Tacna; twelve days later, the port of Arica fell to the Chileans.

Efforts by mediators from the United States failed to put a stop to the bloody conflict late in 1880. Chile sent an army of 25,000 to Lima. By mid-January 1881, Chilean forces had crushed the Peruvian defenders and Lima was an occupied city. Although guerrilla warfare continued sporadically after the fall of Peru's capital, the war's outcome had been decided. The conflict, which had begun as a war between Chile and Bolivia, ultimately placed the heaviest human and financial burden on Peru. Both allies, however, paid a steep price in terms of land lost, for Chile exacted a harsh settlement on its northern neighbors.

By virtue of the Treaty of Ancón, signed on October 23, 1883, Peru ceded the province of Tarapacá to Chile and agreed to a ten-year administration and occupation by its foe of the cities of Arica and Tacna. In March 1884, Bolivia signed a truce with Chile. It stipulated that Antofagasta would pass to Chilean control and that Chile, in turn, would allow Bolivia free access for its goods through the now Chilean-controlled port of Arica. Bolivia and Chile did not sign a peace treaty until 1904.

The War of the Pacific had a tremendous impact on the three belligerents. In its aftermath, Bolivia and Peru were left deeply scarred, in both human and territorial terms. Chile had increased its area by fully one third at the expense of its foes: Peru had lost a substantial part of its southern territory; Bolivia had lost land as well as its access to the Pacific, and it has been landlocked ever since. The war proved to be an economic bonanza for Chile and added to the nation's pantheon of heroes. Almost 125 years after the outbreak of the war, Chile, Bolivia, and Peru are still feeling the effects of the struggle. In 1979, on the hundredth anniversary of the beginning of the war, Peru's military threatened to unleash a war of retribution and reconquest against Chile, and Chileans prepared for renewed conflict. The threat never materialized, and although relations have been tense and precarious on several occasions, Chile, Bolivia, and Peru continue to maintain a civil, although unsettled, relationship.

Another long-lasting effect of the War of the Pacific was the development of a military elite. Chile acquired the services of a German lieutenant colonel, Emil Körner, who was instrumental in the government's founding of the Academia de Guerra (War College) in 1886, with the stated purpose of improving the quality of Chile's officer corps. Under Körner's leadership, the Chilean military became highly professional and modern, along the lines of the Prussian model which had been so effective during the Franco-Prussian War of 1870. The War of the Pacific proved to be an important watershed in Chile's history: a relatively small country had achieved an unexpected military status. The relationship between civil and military authority had reached a turning point and would prove fateful.

President Aníbal Pinto (1876–1881) saw the War of the Pacific from its beginning to near its end. His successor, Domingo Santa María (1881–1886), presided over the war's end and the signing of the peace treaty with Peru and the truce with Bolivia. Chile's substantial military growth provided the forces with which to pacify the Araucanians, who had continued to struggle against the new nation. By the late 1880s, most strife between Indians and the rest of Chile's population had effectively ceased. Under Santa María, the control that the Church had continued to exert over all civil matters was further weakened. Secularization grew as laws created civil authority over previously religious matters such as marriages, birth certifications, and lay cemeteries, many of these ideals promulgated by O'Higgins and his supporters in the 1820s. All that remained to be done was the actual separation of Church and state, which occurred at the end of the first quarter of the twentieth century.

Domingo Santa María was succeeded by José Manuel Balmaceda (1886–1891), former member of Congress and a minister in Santa María's cabinet, over the strong opposition of the Conservative party. The first part of Balmaceda's term was tranquil and productive. The president promoted public education, built schools in many of the country's cities, and founded the Instituto Pedagógico (Normal School), whose main objective was the training of teachers for the secondary school system. He brought German teachers to Chile and created a new concentric system which stressed the interrelationship of the subjects taught, thus replacing the old method of teaching that was centered around unconnected disciplines. He also began the construction of the Internado Nacional Barros Arana (Barros Arana National Boarding School).

In 1888, Captain Policarlo Toro, aboard the transport *Angamos*, took possession of Isla de Pascua (Easter Island), located some 2,000 miles off the Chilean coast. Chile has maintained sovereignty over the island ever since. Rapa Nui, as Easter Island is known by its native population, is the site of the famous *moais*, the giant volcanic rock heads that give the island their imposing appearance.

Communications were greatly improved during Balmaceda's term. Roads, railroads, and telegraph lines were extended to reach greater portions of the national territory. One of the most imposing feats of architecture was the Malleco viaduct, a daring engineering work that went into service in 1890. Designed by a Chilean engineer, Aurelio Lastarria, it was 102 meters (340 feet) high and 347 meters (close to 1,150 feet) long. It is said that the mathematical calculations that went into the construction of this viaduct helped Gustave Eiffel in the building of his famous tower at about the same time. This period of great material and intellectual growth, however, was marred by a civil war, the most disastrous that Chile has ever suffered.

The Civil War of 1891 and Its Aftermath

One year before the end of his term of office, Balmaceda became involved in a constitutional crisis that led to civil war. The opposition had attained a majority of the seats in Congress, and since Chile had an essentially parliamentary system of government, the legislature could oversee the executive to the point of censuring it and depriving it of its right to produce a budget. When this happened, Balmaceda assumed a dictatorial role; the opposition declared itself in revolt, with the support and backing of the navy. An edict was promulgated that declared Balmaceda had been deposed for having violated the Constitution. A junta was organized under the joint control of Jorge Montt, commander of the navy, Ramón Barros Luco, president of the Chamber of Deputies (equivalent of the House in the U.S. Congress), and Waldo Silva, vice president of the Senate. After bitter clashes at Concón and Placilla, on August 21 and 28, 1891, respectively, between supporters and enemies of the executive branch, Balmaceda realized that the struggle was lost. He turned executive command over to General Manuel Baquedano, hero of the War of the Pacific, and took refuge at the Argentine embassy. There, he waited until the last day of his constitutional term of office. On that day, September 19, 1891, he took his life by shooting himself with a pistol. The Civil War of 1891 came to an end. A prominent statue honors Balmaceda at the Plaza Baquedano (also known as Plaza Italia), where Avenida Bernardo O'Higgins becomes Avenida Providencia.

The years between 1891 and 1924 were relatively stable for Chilean politics. There was orderly succession to the presidency, with seven executives serving one five-year term each, although two presidents died from natural causes before finishing their mandates.

An issue which had not been resolved after the wars of independence was the question of the national borders between Chile and Argentina. In 1881, both countries had agreed to set their common border at the continental divide, the point where rivers flowed either to the Pacific (Chile) or to the Atlantic (Argentina). During the presidency of Federico Errázuriz Echaurren (1896–1901), the differences in interpretation of that agreement almost led the two nations to war. Argentina had maintained that the border should be set at the line that joins the highest points on the Andes.

War was averted when both nations agreed to resolve the conflict through the arbitration of the Prince of Wales (the future Edward VII) of Great Britain. In 1899, President Errázuriz and President Julio Roca of Argentina met in the Chilean city of Punta Arenas, where they formally accepted the prince's offer to mediate. Edward VII's judgment, promulgated in 1902, was accepted by both nations. To commemorate the agreement, Chile and Argentina erected the statue *Christ the Redeemer* at (also known as Christ of the Andes) the Uspallata Pass, at an altitude of 3,848 meters (close to 12,700 feet), as a symbol of peace between the two nations. There were disputes concerning other points along the border shared by the two nations throughout the rest of the twentieth century, however, which would test the two countries' resolve.

President Arturo Alessandri Palma

Arturo Alessandri Palma (1868–1950) served as president from 1920 to 1925, after a very narrow victory over Luis Barros Borgoño. As has often been the case in Chilean presidential elections, Alessandri's scant margin forced the Congress to appoint a "tribunal of honor" which decided the election in favor of Alessandri. An upper-middle-class attorney, Alessandri had had ample political experience in Congress before his election to the highest office in the land. During the first three years of his administration, he supported legislation that favored the nation's workers and women's civil rights. The Banco Central (Central Bank) was created during this period. During his administration, the still-unresolved problem of the former Peruvian provinces of Tacna and Arica, under Chilean administration since the end of the War of the Pacific, was placed under the arbitration of the president of the United States. Although the American judgment seemed to favor Chile, a vote was not carried out until 1929. Arica became a permanent part of Chile, and Tacna reverted to Peru. The recognized border between Peru and Chile is in the Azapa Valley, just north of the city of Arica, between the 18th and 19th parallels.

During Alessandri's first few years in office, friction between the executive and legislative branches and the military led to continued disagreements. In 1924, Alessandri presented Congress with his resignation as president but Congress refused to accept it. Instead, the legislative branch offered him the opportunity to absent himself from Chile for six months, and Alessandri accepted.

Alessandri was recalled to the presidency in March 1925, and was received with great enthusiasm. The president dedicated himself to the process of constitutional reform, and on August 30, 1925, a plebiscite was held to vote on the new document. The new constitution was approved and officially adopted on September 18, 1925, remaining in effect for the next forty-eight years. The new code allotted greater powers to the executive branch and prevented the Congress from removing members of the cabinet. Further, it allowed for direct elections by the citizenry, thus making the selection of the chief executive a truly participatory, national event. It also made the separation of Church and state official and fixed the presidential term of office at six years, with immediate reelection to the office ruled unconstitutional. On October 1, 1925, Arturo Alessandri resigned from office and was replaced by the vice president for the rest of the term.

In spite of the enactment of the Constitution of 1925, a great degree of instability remained in the government for a number of years. A series of presidents occupied the highest office in the land from 1925 until 1932, some for extremely short periods of time, most of them resigning or being forced to step down by factions of the government or armed forces. Finally, the state of anarchy came to an end, and political stability returned with the reelection of Arturo Alessandri (1932–1938). The relative stability that had been a hallmark of the Chilean political scene, beginning with the birth of the nation, was again in evidence from 1932 through 1970. Chile was the only Latin American nation that enjoyed active, multiparty politics without assassinations, coups, or revolutions.

President Eduardo Frei Montalva

In 1949, women gained the right to vote, and they exercised that right to vote for president in the elections of 1952. Their vote was crucial in the 1964 election, when Eduardo Frei Montalva, the founder and leader of the Christian Democratic party, was vying for the nation's highest office against several other candidates, among them Salvador Allende Gossens. In 1964, Frei won the presidency, receiving Chile's first majority ever (some 56 percent of all votes) in the race for that office, in great measure due to women's overwhelming vote in his favor.

Frei's administration was characterized by his and his party's attempts to carry out a so-called Revolution in Liberty. Educational reform opened registration to all children of school age, and agrarian reform was promoted but advanced too slowly to effect the changes that would have equalized social and material disparities that had characterized Chile's society since before its independence.

In 1969, Frei's administration nationalized the copper industry, coining the term *chilenización* (Chileanization) of the nation's most important producer of foreign exchange. When his term of office ended in 1970, Chile's political and social scene had become significantly polarized. The presidential elections that year severely tested the mettle of the nation, for in spite of the concerted efforts of the Frei administration to reduce the economic and social disparities that existed in Chilean society, the struggle between those who felt the country was making significant progress to remedy social ills and those who felt that the rate of process should be significantly increased, placed Chile at a crossroads and, ultimately, in the world's consciousness for the rest of the twentieth century.

The Popular Unity Government (1970–1973)

Three principal candidates vied for the nation's highest office in 1970. Dr. Salvador Allende Gossens, a physician by training but a politician since early in life, was the candidate of the Unidad Popular (Popular Unity, or UP), a coalition of leftist parties, chief among them the Socialist (Allende's own) and Communist parties. Other, smaller parties joined these two and increased the chances that Allende could become a significant contender. The poet Pablo Neruda, who had been the candidate of the Communist party, had abandoned that position to give his support to his friend Allende. The MIR, the Movimiento de la Izquierda Revolucionaria (Movement of the Revolutionary Left), was a splinter group that, until it joined the Unidad Popular, had been a guerrilla movement operating outside the law.

Running under the banner of the Partido Nacional (National Party), a conservative party, was Jorge Alessandri Rodríguez, president from 1958 to 1964 and the son of a former president, Arturo Alessandri, who had earned the respect of the people of Chile during his term of office but had not been able to strengthen the nation against the growing ravages of inflation and social inequalities. Aged seventy-four in 1970, Alessandri was a conservative at a time when the nation was impatient for change. Third was the standard-bearer for the Christian Democrats, Radomiro Tomic, who espoused the completion of agrarian reform and held political views that were to the left of his party's centrist tendencies and, thus, were not radically different from those of the Unidad Popular. During his campaign, Tomic reserved his harshest criticism for Alessandri, at times seeming to promote the idea that a victory by the Unidad Popular, if not by him, would create the possibility for effecting real and fundamental social change.

When the election took place, Salvador Allende received 1,070,344 votes, or 36.3 percent of the votes cast (versus 977,902, or 39.5 percent, in the election of 1964, when he had lost to Frei). Alessandri obtained 1,031,159 votes, or 34.9 percent, and Tomic, 821,801, or 27.8 percent. (The figures do not add up exactly because there were other minor candidates.) Only 39,185 votes separated Allende and Alessandri, and since no candidate had received a majority, Congress had the right to choose between the two candidates who received the highest number of votes.

In the past, when faced with similar circumstances, Congress had chosen the candidate with the plurality. In 1970, however, the situation was unique: never before had the candidate with the plurality been a Marxist who openly promoted the creation of a socialist society via democratic means. Before the election, polls had suggested that had Frei been eligible to run for a second consecutive term, he would have won the election handily. With this in mind, Alessandri offerred the Congress the following carrot: if it chose him over Allende, he would resign immediately after his designation as president, thus allowing for new elections, with Frei likely to win.

Some Christian Democrats liked the plan, but Tomic and most of the party's congressional representatives opposed it. Instead, they demanded passage of a list of constitutional guarantees that Allende would have to sign and abide by in order to be designated the winner of the election. Among these guarantees were support of the multiparty system, maintenance of civil liberties, freedom of the press, access by all to the nation's television stations, protection for the military from the creation of militias, and other rights enjoyed under previous administrations and seen to be either nonexistent or greatly diminished in other nations under Marxist governments.

The Congress found itself pressured by all sides, both internal and external, to assure that Allende would or would not be selected to the presidency. The extreme left threatened violence if he were not, although the Congress, constitutionally, could decide for Allende or Alessandri. The opposition, supported by those who could not envision or stomach a Marxist president, even one who had been freely elected, and by foreign sources (prominent among them the U.S. government, with Henry Kissinger actively involved, and the CIA [Central Intelligence Agency]), struggled to find some means whereby the Congress would ultimately decide for Alessandri.

Two days before Congress was to make its judgment, extreme right-wing groups, allegedly supported by the CIA, attempted to carry out the kidnapping of the commander in chief of Chile's army, René Schneider. Their aim was to blame the leftist MIR or the Popular Unity coalition, thus swaying the Christian Democratic members of Congress and convincing them to vote against Allende. Schneider resisted the attempt and was mortally wounded in the ensuing gun battle. He died one day after the Congress voted to confirm Allende as president. On November 3, 1970, Salvador Allende was inaugurated as president of Chile for the term that covered the period 1970–1976.

There is no period in Chilean history that has been as thoroughly studied and debated as that of the Popular Unity government of Salvador Allende, which lasted from November 3, 1970, until the early morning hours of September 11, 1973. The support that Allende had after the election, some 36.3 percent of the electorate, grew to as much as 40 percent but never higher. At the same time, the opposition, both in Congress and in the electorate, remained adamantly opposed to the administrative, social, and economic policies espoused by the UP.

Demonstrations, both in support of and in opposition to the government, became almost daily occurrences. Governments abroad supported one side or the other, depending on their own political realities and perspectives. Reality in Chile itself took on an almost surrealistic tone. The inconsistencies of both capitalism and socialism became evident. As the state of the economy worsened, the left laid the blame squarely on the intransigence of the opposition and on the efforts by powerful interests abroad, mainly originating in the United States: President Richard Nixon, Secretary of State Henry Kissinger, and the Central Intelligence Agency. The 60 percent of the Congress and electorate, however, saw the worsening economy as a sign of the failure of socialism.

September 11, 1973

The stalemate grew worse and, ultimately, led to a constitutional crisis that reached its climax the morning of September 11, 1973. The armed forces, under the command of their respective leaders, launched a highly effective and brutal attack on the Moneda, the government palace where President Allende had taken refuge. The army surrounded the structure, a large building occupying a square block in downtown Santiago, located between the Alameda Bernardo O'Higgins and Moneda, streets that run from east to west, and Teatinos and Morandé, which run from north to south. As the army fired on the building from the ground, the air force bombed it from the air. Reporters watched the action from the Carrera, a luxury hotel located at the intersection of Teatinos and Agustinas, one block away with a clear view of the Moneda. (The area between Moneda and Teatinos is an open square, the Plaza de la Constitución.)

Salvador Allende, who had declared that he would not step down as president, as the military had demanded, died in the assault on the palace. The left immediately stated that he had been assassinated by the military; the opposition maintained that the president, who had, according to some sources, stated that he would take his life rather than surrender, had committed suicide. Today, even critics of the coup tend to acknowledge that the evidence strongly indicates that President Salvador Allende, facing the inevitable end of his mandate, made the decision to take his life rather than surrender his constitutional post. The move reminded many of his predecessor Balmaceda, who took his own life on the last day of his mandate, in 1891.

The armed forces quickly consolidated their control of the nation, both politically and economically. Although most independent polls at the time seemed to indicate broad support for the coup, given the state of the economy and the growing polarization of Chile's people, almost no one was prepared for the ferocity and excesses of the takeover. The opposition parties expected that the military would return control of the government to civilians after an initial purging of the leftist coalition. The armed forces had a different plan in mind. When called upon by opposition groups in Congress to restore the constitutional order, the military responded by dissolving the legislative body, curtailing the activities of those members who had opposed the Unidad Popular, and outlawing all leftist parties.

The army commander, General Augusto Pinochet Ugarte, quickly assumed a leading role within the military junta that controlled the government. The air force commander, Gustavo Leigh, the navy's Admiral José

Toribio Medina, and General César Mendoza Durán, general director of the *carabineros*, Chile's militarized national police, took a secondary role to Pinochet. Together, the members of the junta justified their *pronunciamiento* (pronouncement), as they euphemistically called the coup d'état, by alleging that a "Plan Zeta [Z]," a plot to systematically murder members of the opposition to the Unidad Popular, both political and civilian, had existed at the time of the coup, a plan thwarted only by the quick action of the military on September 11. Whether such a plot was a fact or an excuse for the actions taken may never be ascertained fully.

The junta provided graphic details, including photos of armaments purportedly being amassed by the left to carry out such a plot. It reminded the nation that a large number of crates had arrived at Santiago's airport in 1972, and had been allowed to bypass customs. It stated that those crates contained the armaments later displayed by the military at the principal home of Salvador Allende. The armed forces also pointed out that the weapons exhibited shortly after the coup were all from Eastern bloc countries, not from Chile's arsenal.

The left stated that the armaments had been planted by the armed forces in an attempt to convince Chile, and the world, that its actions had been timely and just. As the distance between the events that began on September 11 and the present grows, details continue to emerge that support both the junta's allegations and provide evidence of its brutality, and the complicity of foreign interests, especially of the United States.

On the day of the coup, a general curfew was declared throughout the nation; it remained in effect for several years, although its severity was modified as the military strengthened its hold on the reins of government, and active opposition to the new order weakened and mostly disappeared. Opposition leaders left the country, either of their own accord or under pressure from the new government. The majority went into exile in the United States or western Europe, and from there they continued their opposition to the junta. On December 16, 1974, General Augusto Pinochet was officially named president of Chile, a post that he was to hold for fifteen years.

Clearly, during the first two years of the military dictatorship, the junta appeared to have the support of the majority of Chileans, who strongly wished to see the restoration of political order and the reconstruction of the economy. The lawlessness and anarchy that had been in evidence during the years from 1970 to 1973 did diminish appreciably. Civil rights, however, experienced the strict control that always accompanies the imposition of military government.

General Pinochet pointed out that Chile's victory over communism had international significance. Henceforth, Chile would carry out a total transformation of society so that Marxism would never again take root. The rest of the world, in his view, would do well to emulate Chile in its successful eradication of communism. Although the excesses of the military takeover and subsequent control of the government were increasingly turning Chile into a pariah in the eyes of the world, it was an economic program, actually begun decades earlier, which began to focus the world's attention on Chile.

During the 1950s, many Chileans had studied at the University of Chicago, or in Chile under academicians who had received advanced professional education there, and as part of an exchange program between that American university and Chile's Catholic University. These Chilean economists were soon called "the Chicago Boys" or neoliberal economists.

Neoliberal economists espoused the philosophy that the inefficient allocation of resources resulted from the politicization of the economy, over-regulation, protectionism, and the growing state control of the nation's basic industries. Also, for decades the state had increasingly made promises which could not be kept because of the economic policies it actively espoused.

In April 1975, Minister of Finance Jorge Cauas announced an economic shock program that the government felt would eradicate the country's more than seventy years of inflation, which by September 1973 had rendered the *escudo*, Chile's currency, practically worthless. Some 80,000 government employees lost their jobs and unemployment grew throughout the economy; industrial output dropped 25 percent. However, inflation dropped from 300 percent in 1974 to 84 percent in 1977. The government's deficit practically disappeared by the end of 1975.

During the first years of the new order, unemployment remained high, and the gap between haves and have-nots grew. Although store shelves quickly became full, many were unable to afford the goods which were displayed. Any discontent, however, was not openly voiced due to the military's strict control.

In 1980, the government initiated a national plebiscite, in which Pinochet wished to institutionalize the program of socioeconomic and political change that the military had implemented. A new constitution, strongly managed by the Pinochet government, was implemented in 1981. In it, Pinochet's term as president was extended until 1989.

Late in the winter of 1988, an open plebiscite was held throughout the nation. Voters had two choices: a *sí* vote would allow Pinochet to remain as president for the term (1989–1997); a *no* vote would allow for open, free elections. Pinochet could, under such elections, be a candidate, but in a field that would include opposition. When the plebiscite was held, the *no* votes accounted for 56 percent of the electorate. Pinochet received a substantial 44 percent but agreed to abide by those results.

From 1989 to the Present

In December 1989, free elections for president were held, and Patricio Aylwin, a Christian Democrat, was elected for one four-year term. Pinochet remained as commander in chief of the armed forces until March 1998, when he stepped down and retired from the army. Later that year, under the 1981 Constitution, Pinochet became senator for life and took his place in the Chilean Senate.

Aylwin remained in office until 1993, and although there was much support for amending the Constitution to allow him to run again, he declined to do so. That same year, Eduardo Frei Ruiz-Tagle, the Christian Democrat son of previous president Eduardo Frei Montalva (1964–1970), was elected president with a majority of the vote that essentially matched that of his father in 1964 (55 percent), for a six-year term that ran from 1994 through 2000.

Today, Chile and the world marvel at the stability and strength of the country's economy even as the brutal excesses of the military dictatorship remain in evidence and come under the closer scrutiny allowed by the return of democratic rule. The nation, with a population of close to 15 million, is Latin America's little economic giant, and its economic policies are being emulated by the rest of the Latin American continent and beyond.

2

Religion

LIKE THE REST of Spanish America, Chile has been at least nominally Roman Catholic since its colonial beginnings in the mid-1500s. By royal statute, Spanish conquistadors established a church in every part of the colony that had a population of at least 300 inhabitants. Since only Spanish citizens could legally emigrate to the Spanish New World, the Church was able to maintain both a de facto and a de jure monopoly on the spreading of Christianity. There was great religious and political ferment in sixteenth-century Europe, beginning with Luther's reformation in Germany and Henry VIiI's break with Rome in England. Spain effectively kept non-Roman Catholic Christian sects from spreading across its colonies until the nineteenth century, when immigration from others parts of Europe, especially Germany and Great Britain, and proselytizing of Protestant denominations from the United States, began to add to the religious melting pot.

Given the relatively small indigenous population of Chile, especially compared to that of other Spanish American colonies such as Peru, Bolivia, Guatemala, and Mexico, and the absence of significant numbers of African slaves, the Church did not have to contend with other religious influences in the spread of its teachings. In many places, instead of simply crushing non-Christian faiths, the Church attempted to combine opposing beliefs and customs, as it had done in Guatemala, Peru, and Bolivia, through the fusion of Christianity and indigenous religions. The parallel process that arose especially in the Caribbean, with the infusion of Africans and the various faiths they brought with them, did not occur in Chile. Thus, the Roman Catholic

San Marcos Church, in Chile's northernmost city, Arica, designed by the French engineer, Gustave Eiffel (1832–1923), in 1868.

Church enjoyed almost complete supremacy in the spread of Christianity for 300 years.

During the period beginning with the wars of independence (1810–1818), a gradual but significant change occurred in the Roman Catholic Church's predominance in daily life. Many of the patriots supported a liberalism that sought to loosen the strict control exercised by the Church over lay affairs. Attempts were made to create nonreligious cemeteries and schools that were not under the strict administration of the Church. The more conservative elements of society, among them landholders and some politicians, sought to limit the influence of these liberalizing forces and to maintain the strong bonds that existed between the Church and government.

Perhaps two factors contributed to the gradual separation between the Church and the state that became official in 1925. The influences of the founding patriots, with their desire to liberalize the society which was being created, and of non-Spanish ethnic groups, chiefly British and German settlers, had a growing and significant effect on Church-state relations.

Early on, Bernardo O'Higgins attempted to separate the state from the Church. Ambrosio O'Higgins, his father, and others of British and Irish ancestry—the Mackennas, Cochranes, O'Briens, Millers, and Williamses, to name only a few—have figured prominently in Chilean history. A city map of Santiago reveals an abundance of such names among its many streets. All of these important, non-Spanish-surnamed individuals, whether Catholic or not, influenced the religious makeup of the nation, bringing new ideas to bear upon the mind-set of Chilean society.

The government began to seriously encourage the immigration of non-Spanish people, especially Germans, around the middle of the nineteenth century. Significant numbers continued to arrive until close to the end of that century, with many settling in the areas south of Santiago, all the way to Puerto Montt and even beyond.

The majority of the English who settled in Chile, especially along the central coast, brought their Anglican faith. German settlers either reinforced Catholicism or brought Lutheranism to their new home. By 1880, the Roman Catholic Church was increasingly permitting the union of German Lutherans and native Chilean Catholics. The Roman Catholic Church's predominant influence was not greatly threatened since Anglicanism and Lutheranism mostly served the English and German communities, respectively, and made no attempt to proselytize beyond them.

In the twentieth century a more diverse group of Protestants began to arise, most of them as a result of the proselytizing efforts of missionaries from the United States. American missionaries began to make inroads among Roman Catholics who were dissatisfied with the established church. Many non-Catholic Christian groups are now firmly established, among them Seventh-Day Adventists, Evangelicals, Mormons, Methodists, Presbyterians, and Baptists.

The Roman Catholic Church has also undergone changes, beginning especially during the 1960s, as a result of Vatican II and the growing radicalization of the political scene not only in Chile but also in the rest of Latin America.

Until the twentieth century, the Roman Catholic Church had opposed the separation of Church and state. The alliance between them had existed for hundreds of years, beginning with Constantine's establishment of Christianity as the official religion of the Roman Empire. The Reformation had altered this bond, but the Roman church maintained its power among European Catholic nations, using the union as a bond of protection from Protestant incursions. A similar pattern was brought to the New World by both Spain and Portugal in the sixteenth century.

In Chile, the years between 1920 and 1925 proved to be crucial in the breaking of these bonds. The official separation between Church and state was carried out in 1925, under the new constitution. The smooth transition was a result of several factors. There was a relative indifference within Chilean society toward religious matters, and the archbishop of Santiago, Crescente Errázuriz, used his ample skills to effect a ready acceptance of the separation by the Church hierarchy. Thus, the Church in Chile avoided some of the conflict which disestablishment had occasioned in other nominally Catholic countries, such as France, Portugal, Mexico, and Uruguay, in the preceding twenty years.

In June 1925, the new constitution recognized the legality and historical relevance of the Roman Catholic Church but also allowed the free exercise of all religions and recognized the right of these other religious groups to own property and erect buildings. The government approved a five-year period of transition during which it continued to support the Roman church while the Church sought private sources of support.

The period from 1925 until the late 1950s was one of social ferment. The traditional alliance between the Church hierarchy and conservative forces had been weakening throughout the nineteenth century and the early decades of the twentieth. Even as the leadership of the Church continued to support conservative ideologies, parish priests increasingly allied themselves with the poor, perceiving a growing need for social change. This movement within the Church, which supported a role for social change with religious backing, became known as Liberation Theology. Throughout Latin America, clergy such as Camilo Torres in Colombia, Ernesto Cardenal and Miguel D'Escoto in Nicaragua, and Archbishop Oscar Romero in El Salvador, actively supported those whom they felt had not enjoyed the fruits of the societies to which they belonged. The Vatican, even as it supported the move toward social change, criticized any political involvement on the part of its clergy.

Catholic missionaries from the United States, especially those belonging to the Maryknoll order, became actively involved in social reform in Chile and other parts of Latin America; Cardenal and D'Escoto were both members of that American religious order. Schools were founded in Santiago, St. George's being perhaps the best known. Liberal Roman Catholic and more conservative Protestant missionaries from the United States both began to vie for the allegiance of those who had become dissatisfied with their religious circumstances and experiences.

A new party, the Christian Democrats, whose modern origins are to be found in western Europe after the end of World War II, came to the forefront in Latin America in the late 1950s and early 1960s. In Chile, they rose to predominance under Eduardo Frei Montalva, who promised a middle road between conservatives and leftists. When he ran for the highest office in 1964, he received the first majority of the electorate in Chile's history, some 56 percent. In very general terms, the party espoused social and economic reform within the tenets of Christianity, as a way of rejecting the advancing radicalization of Chilean society, especially as promoted by Marxist parties such as the Communists and Socialists and their more extreme offshoots. Frei's six-year term produced some agrarian reform and the beginnings of income redistribution, but not the significant reorganization of Chile's economy and society that had been promised and forecast. With Allende's election in 1970, the Christian Democrats were relegated to being a segment of the opposition to the Popular Unity coalition that had supported Allende's candidacy and subsequent election as president.

Allende's overthrow, in September 1973, and the military dictatorship that ensued, gave the Catholic Church, both hierarchy and general clergy, the opportunity to provide a protective umbrella for those who were being persecuted by the military government. There were clashes between Church and government, but Pinochet, himself a practicing Roman Catholic, did not react strongly and the Church became both a beacon of hope for those who sought refuge from the excesses of the right and a thorn in the side of the more reactionary elements of society who were torn between their adherence to Catholicism and their political, social, and economic views.

The Roman Catholic Church in Chile has become a religious body that is more representative of Chilean society as a whole, no longer allying itself only with conservative elements. Many Catholics, whether nominal or practicing, generally respect the tenets of their church even as they reject some of the more rigidly conservative views of the Vatican, among them the prohibition of artificial birth control, marriage of the clergy, and to some extent abortion.

More than 80 percent of Chileans are at least nominally Roman Catholic. Attendance at Sunday Mass varies but is certainly not as large as it is in the United States. More women are in evidence than men, but all maintain varying ties to the Church, beginning with baptism and continuing with other sacraments such as marriage and last rites. The competition occasioned not by mainline Protestant sects, such as the Anglican and Lutheran churches, but by the growing influence of the Evangelical denominations that have entered mainly from the United States, has given the Roman Catholic Church a new impetus to widen its influence in all aspects of its parishioners' lives. Liberation Theology, with its focus on social issues, has also attracted back some of those who had seen the Church as an ally of the aristocracy.

3

Social Customs

NATIONAL HOLIDAYS

THE ORIGINAL NATURE of Chile as a Roman Catholic nation is reflected in its observance of religious feast days along with state holidays, even after the separation of Church and state that occurred in 1925. The nation places these celebrations, both lay and religious, under the category of "public feasts." Chronologically, the following holidays are celebrated at the national level: New Year's Day, January 1; Good Friday, Holy Saturday, and Easter Sunday, on the appointed days in either March or April; Labor Day, May 1; May 21, in commemoration of the naval battle of Iquique, in 1879; August 15, the Assumption of the Virgin Mary; September 18, Independence Day; September 19, Army Day; October 12 (known variously as Día de la Hispanidad [Hispanism Day], the more common term used in Spain; Día de la Raza [loosely, "Day of the Race," for the ethnic groups (Spaniards, Indians, Africans) that arose beginning with Columbus's coming to America], the most common term used throughout the New World; or "Discovery of America," less used today because of criticism of Columbus and Spain's conquest of America, and of the correctness of the term "discovery")). All Saints' Day, on November 1; the Feast of the Immaculate Conception, on December 8; and Christmas Day, on December 25, round out the holidays.

New Year's Day is celebrated in Chile much as it is in the rest of the world. Some choose to greet the beginning of the new year by attending parties that continue into New Year's Day. Others choose to be with their families first and to move on to social celebrations later on. Since New Year's Day in this southernmost part of the southern hemisphere is within two weeks of the beginning of summer, many celebrations are held outdoors, although summer evenings can be somewhat cool.

May 21 is a major holiday because it is the anniversary of the naval battle of Iquique, in 1879. Although Chile essentially lost that battle—for the corvette *Esmeralda* was sunk by the Peruvian ship *Huáscar*, with the loss of many lives—the event created the nation's most renowned naval hero, Captain Arturo Prat. On May 21, 1960, a major earthquake devastated a large portion of the nation's center. Some feel that the fact that this natural disaster occurred at the beginning of the day, and on a national holiday, helped to keep casualties lower than they would have been had more people been out in the areas which suffered the collapse of buildings and other structures. Valparaíso has an impressive monument that commemorates the naval battle.

September 18 is the day when Chile declared its independence from Spain in 1810. Chileans celebrate the holiday quite boisterously, with parties, both private and public. The national dance, the *cueca*, is a staple that day, as is the consumption of typical foods, washed down with world-renowned Chilean wine. Since September 18 falls within two or three days of the official end of winter, Chileans consider it the unofficial beginning of spring, much as Americans consider Labor Day to mark the unofficial end of summer.

On September 19, Chile's military continues to celebrate the nation's independence with a colorful parade along some of Santiago's main avenues. It is an event that most children enjoy at least once during their early years and that they remember fondly as they grow up. The advent of television has surely affected the crowds that line Santiago's streets, for today it is possible to watch the endless waves of disciplined marchers from the comfort of one's home.

After the military coup of September 11, 1973, when the armed forces overthrew the elected government of Socialist President Salvador Allende, the event was officially commemorated by the military government. When a section of Avenida Providencia, one of Santiago's main streets, was made one-way from the uptown part of the city toward city center, a new segment was opened in the opposite direction. It received two names, Nueva Providencia (New Providence), and Avenida Once de Septiembre (September 11 Avenue). Thus, people of divergent political views could refer to this new artery as they deemed fit. There has recently been an effort to disassociate the day from its political and historical implications. Some have pushed to disconnect the day from any celebration of the "pronouncement," as the military liked to call the coup. The military has suggested that September 11 or a date close to it be declared a "day of reconciliation." No consensus has yet been reached.

During the Franco dictatorship in Spain (1939–1975), his government created *El Día de la Hispanidad* (Hispanism Day), celebrated on October 12, in an effort to broaden the concept that Spain and its former colonies in America shared a common history and culture. After Franco's death in November 1975, the day ceased to be celebrated in Spain. Spanish America continues to commemorate the day in varying degrees, depending on the relationship that each nation perceives it has with its Spanish inheritance. Chile is among those that continue to celebrate the day officially, with the closing of offices and schools and scattered activities that promote its cultural ties with Spain. The intense polemic provoked by commemoration of the 500th anniversary of Columbus's arrival in the New World, in 1992, might yet occasion a change in this national holiday in Chile and in the rest of Spanish America, although Chileans celebrate both their Hispanic and their Indian inheritances.

All Saints' Day, November 1, is a religious day observed by many Christian churches. On November 2, many people visit cemeteries to place flowers at the graves of loved ones.

Christmas Day falls, of course, on December 25, but for many Chileans the celebration really begins the preceding day. It is then that children open their gifts, as close to midnight as their ages permit, and families gather to enjoy a great meal as the prelude to the opening of gifts. Many children would probably say that Christmas Day is December 24, for that is the day which they remember as the culmination of all of their days and days of expectant hope. Those who put up Christmas trees usually do so on Christmas Eve, following a tradition that began in Europe.

Some choose to attend the *misa del gallo* (midnight Mass; literally, the cock's Mass), after which they return home for more celebration. On December 25, most people visit extended family or friends. Since Christmas falls very close to the summer solstice, the weather is warm and many people enjoy soccer games, picnics, and backyard meals. Christmas marks the official beginning of summer, and many *santiaguinos* begin to plan their vacations, which they typically spend at one of the many beaches along Chile's coast.

CUISINE

Chile's cuisine is as varied and colorful as its culture and its natural setting. Its indigenous and Spanish origins and its long coastline have given the country an abundance and diversity of foods that are tempting to the palate.

As in the rest of the American continent, corn (*maíz* in Spanish but known as *choclo* in Chile and the rest of the Southern Cone) is the basic ingredient of many of the foods that trace their origin to the first inhabitants of Chile, the Araucanians or Mapuches, and the Aymaras and Incas who once conquered the northern half of the country. This contribution to the national cuisine, which has its origins in Mexico, is now as native to Chile as it is to the rest of the continent.

One national dish is called *humitas*. These corn-based treats are found in Peru as well, and some varieties can bear a striking resemblance to tamales as prepared in Mexico. The basic ingredients are puréed corn, powdered sugar, and salt. *Humitas*, once puréed, are wrapped in a package made of corn husks and steamed or simmered in water. To eat them, one unwraps the corn husks and sprinkles powdered sugar on the puréed corn, which has acquired the shape of the packaging. The mixture of the salty and the sweet provides an interesting and rewarding treat.

Whereas *humitas* are normally made entirely of native American ingredients, *pastel de choclo* is an amalgam of ingredients that reflect both Indian and European origins. It is a corn pie that contains beef, chicken, raisins, onion, olives, garlic, chili (known as *ají* in Chile), cumin, olive oil, salt, and powdered or granulated sugar. Other ingredients are sometimes added. *Pastel de choclo* has sugar sprinkled on top before it is baked, so that it forms a brownish crust.

Empanadas (turnovers) are found throughout the Spanish-speaking world. They can have varying fillings and can be deep-fried or baked. Those that are deep-fried in oil can be filled with cheese, fish, meat, or even fruit, the last used as a dessert. To some, however, the baked *empanada* is the most Chilean of foods. The filling is composed of finely chopped onions; boneless steak cut into quarter-inch cubes or ground beef; seedless raisins that have been soaked in water; sliced hard-boiled eggs; olive oil; chili pepper (although the *empanada* is not usually spicy hot); cumin; black pepper; and water. These ingredients are combined into a mixture that is called *pino* and placed inside pastry dough. Baked *empanadas* are normally substantial in size, reaching a length of five to six inches or more, and can be entire meals by themselves. A meal of *empanadas* is not complete without either a Chilean dry red wine or hot tea to wash them down.

Porotos granados (cranberry beans with squash and corn) is another well-known Chilean dish. If these beans are not available, navy beans can be substituted. To prepare *porotos granados*, one combines the beans, cold water, olive oil, chopped onions, garlic, tomatoes, dried basil, oregano, winter squash, corn kernels, black pepper, and salt. The resulting meal can be served in soup plates, accompanied by a topping called *pebre* (described later).

Cazuela is a substantial soup that can be almost a meal in itself. It is usually made with chicken (*cazuela de ave*), although beef is sometimes substituted;

corn on the cob (cut in thirds); *zapallo*, a type of pumpkin; rice; peas; and carrots. Those who come to the table with a hefty appetite begin their meal with *cazuela* and continue it with *empanadas*. Since each can be a meal in itself, it becomes difficult to decide which one is the *pièce de résistance*, the main course.

Pernil de chanco a la chilena (braised fresh ham with chili sauce) requires a boneless, fresh ham, coarsely chopped onions, chicken stock, finely chopped garlic, olive oil, distilled white vinegar, thinly sliced, peeled carrots, finely chopped bay leaves, fresh red chili, oregano, salt, and water.

The dishes just described are essentially products of the land. The Pacific Ocean, bordering close to 3,000 miles of the landmass on the west, provides a bounty of fish and shellfish for which Chile is world famous. It has been said that there are more than 200 types of seafood available along the coast.

The *centolla*, similar to the Alaskan king crab, is used to prepare *budín de centolla*, a pudding made of crab, butter, finely chopped onions or shallots, flour, light cream, egg yolks, Cayenne pepper, Münster cheese, egg whites, salt, white pepper, and freshly grated Parmesan cheese. Like its northern cousin, the *centolla* is expensive and, from time to time, not available on the market due to government regulations imposed for conservation purposes. The *centolla* can also be eaten with melted butter, condiments, and the standard implements employed to get through the hard shell.

Another crustacean that is much smaller and resembles the Chesapeake Bay blue crab is the *jaiba*. It is found along the central coast and is sometimes sold by fisherman right on the spot, freshly pulled from the cold waters of the Pacific.

Chupe de marisco consists of sea scallops, cut in half crosswise; white wine; finely chopped shallots; fresh bread crumbs; light cream; butter; flour; chili paste (optional); ground nutmeg; Cayenne pepper; salt; ground white pepper; freshly grated Münster cheese; hard-boiled eggs, quartered lengthwise; and long-grain rice. One can substitute *locos* (fresh abalone) for the scallops, to prepare a *chupe de locos*.

Congrio, an eel-like fish, can be made into *caldillo de congrio*. It is a fish, tomato, and potato soup that also contains olive oil, onions, garlic, oregano, bay leaf, cilantro (coriander), and parsley. *Corvina* (sea bass) can be substituted if *congrio* is not available.

On Tenglo Island, off the coast of southern Chile, many savor the *curanto*, a sort of clambake composed of lobsters, crabs, mussels, oysters, potato patties, peas, beans, and a whole suckling pig, all baked for several hours in a pit lined with hot rocks, a common method for cooking outdoors.

Another of the hundreds of shellfish that Chileans enjoy eating is the sea urchin, known as the *erizo*, which is considerably larger than those found on North American beaches; some of them are four inches or larger in diameter. It is not uncommon to see people squeezing lemon juice onto the live urchins and then consuming them. To some they are an acquired taste, but many consider *erizos* a great delicacy.

Chileans like to prepare a type of sauce called *pebre*, quite similar to Mexico's *pico de gallo* (literally, cock's beak), which can accompany almost any kind of food. The main ingredients are olive oil, red or white wine vinegar, water, finely chopped cilantro, chopped onions, red chili paste, garlic, and salt. The amount of chili depends on individual taste: it can be quite mild or eye-watering hot. *Pebre* is a traditional accompaniment to red meat and rice, but it seems to blend well with many other foods. Many restaurants serve *pebre* as a topping for the crusty bread that accompanies one's meal.

Color (literally, color), a sauce made of garlic and paprika, is prepared by heating these two ingredients in melted fat or cooking oil. Chili can be added to the mixture. The orange-red sauce keeps indefinitely and can be added to a variety of foods to give them both taste and color.

Those who lack the time to prepare typical Chilean cuisine can still enjoy meals that are quick to prepare but are a cut or two above fast food. Shorter lunch hours have made many classic sandwiches more popular now than they were earlier. Some of these sandwiches have names that identify their ingredients quite readily; others bear titles which have their origins in history or folklore.

An *ave-palta* (chicken and avocado) sandwich has been a staple for the luncheon crowd for many years. As the name indicates in Spanish, it is a mixture of diced chicken (*ave* is the generic word for "poultry"), avocado (*palta*), and mayonnaise, served on a roll or sliced bread. The *Barros Luco* is a sandwich made with broiled beef and cheese, and served hot. (Ramón Barros Luco was president of Chile from 1910 to 1915.) The *Barros Jarpa* is similar to the *Barros Luco* except that ham is used instead of beef; it, too, is served hot. (Ernesto Barros Jarpa, born late in the nineteenth century, was a writer, attorney, and diplomat who filled several cabinet positions in the government, among them minister of finance, minister of the interior, and minister of foreign relations.) The *chacarero* (a *chacarero* is a farm laborer or field worker) contains broiled beef, tomato, green chili, and green beans. All of these last three sandwiches can be served between two slices of bread or inside a *marraqueta* (loaf), a Chilean bread that is similar in shape, color, and texture to the French baguette.

Chileans are known for having a sweet tooth. Pastry shops abound where one can enjoy excellent cakes (*tortas*), open-face pies (*kuchen*, a word that reflects their German origin), and *queque* (from the English "cake"), a sort of pound or white cake, sometimes served with powdered sugar on top, and a common accompaniment to a cup of coffee or hot tea (usually with milk).

One ingredient which Chileans use in countless desserts and candies is *manjar* (literally, delicacy), also known throughout Latin America as *dulce de leche* (milk sweet). It is essentially a combination of fresh milk and sugar, cooked over a slow fire until the mixture turns a light brown and attains the consistency of very thick molasses. *Manjar* is the most common filling for a cake and is used for many doughnut-like pastries as well. It can be spread on toast, with or instead of butter, and is even dried to a consistency that resembles fudge and sold as candy.

Making *manjar* involves patience and time, since the milk and sugar need to be boiled slowly and stirred fairly often. Those who are impatient or unwilling to spend the time required to make it the old-fashioned way can purchase a can of sweetened, condensed milk, remove the label, and boil the *unopened* can in an open pan for an hour to two hours, making sure that there is always enough water to cover the can. Once the necessary amount of time has passed, the can is removed from the boiling water and left to cool. The contents can then be removed and used. Extra ingredients can be added to the basic milk and sugar, such as almonds or coconut.

The climate in Chile is ideal for the growing of many fruits. Bananas and papayas, for example, can be cultivated in the northern third of the country. The Central Valley, with its Mediterranean climate, devoid of hard freezes in the winter and with summers that are warm and dry, has become a center for the cultivation of peaches, nectarines, apples, oranges, lemons, limes, raspberries, strawberries, melons, watermelons, and the many varieties of grapes for which Chile has long been famous. As one travels south from Santiago, the increasing importance of fruit-growing to the national economy, in terms of both internal consumption and export, is readily evident. Many of these fruits are sold during the winter in American supermarkets. Since seasons are the opposite in the southern hemisphere, there is less competition from fruit growers in the United States, who do not cultivate apples and grapes in April and May, when Chile's Central Valley is enjoying these two months of autumn.

SHOPPING

Supermarket shoppers are accustomed to produce sections that occupy a significant part of the entire store. The necessity for these becomes obvious when one sees the tremendous variety of fruits and vegetables available.

There are a dozen varieties of avocado, from the roughly pear-sized *palta*, green or purple, to the large *palta californiana* (California avocado), which isn't from that U.S. state but simply equal in size to those grown there. Leaf vegetables, onions, and other fresh produce also fill the endless counters as far as the eye can see.

The typical supermarket's delicatessen department offers both ready-to-eat and fresh cuts of meats, cheeses, olives, and other items. This is as much a tradition inherited from Europe as it is an outgrowth of the time when supermarkets were not in existence and shoppers patronized small stores that offered only a few, specialized items. Shoppers are keenly aware that although meats and cheeses are available cut and prepackaged, they also are offered cut to order. Weights are in the metric system, so if one wishes to purchase enough deli meat to make sandwiches, one must ask for, perhaps, 200 to 300 grams (roughly seven to eleven ounces) of ham, roast beef, or cheese.

Since the late 1950s, when supermarkets began to proliferate across Chile, many of the tiny shops have disappeared; their wares now appear in sections of the ever-growing supermarket, which accepts cash, checks, and credit cards. If shoppers are suddenly short of cash, they can usually find a *cajero automático* (ATM machine) on the premises that will provide them with the funds they require.

Youngsters are usually available to assist shoppers in carrying out their groceries (modest tips are most welcome), although it is certainly not frowned upon if one carries one's own purchases. Strategically located, usually as the shopper heads out of the cashier's area, are tempting displays of pastries, cakes, and the like. There are also shops in any city which specialize in such bakery goods. Most of these pastries are veritable works of art.

WINES, SPIRITS, AND A COUNTRY DRINK

A particularly popular aperitif in Chile is the *pisco sour*, an alcoholic drink that has its origins in Peru, specifically in Pisco, a town south of Lima, not far from Ica. Most recipes refer to this drink as Peruvian, but Peru's neighbors from Colombia south have appropriated it for themselves, especially Chile. Many Chileans are probably unaware that *pisco* originated in Peru, and there has even been a move in that country to prevent Chile from using the name *pisco*, in much the same way that France has attempted to enjoin producers of champagne from using that appellation unless the bubbly is produced in the French area that originated it.

Pisco is fermented from the muscatel grape. In Chile, the largest producer of *pisco* is the Capel Company, which has its headquarters in the Elqui Valley, an hour from La Serena, north of Santiago. There are several labels under which Capel sells its *pisco* and it comes in a variety of alcohol concentrations, ranging from 35 percent to 50 percent (70–100 proof). *Pisco* is made by extracting the juice and the pulp from the grape; the fermentation process is begun in large, steel containers. Once the fermentation process is complete, the *pisco* is distilled. The liquid that remains after the fermentation is mixed with water to reduce the alcohol content to the desired level. Finally, it is aged in oak barrels before being bottled for sale.

There are two common ways of consuming *pisco*: the *pisco sour* and the *piscola*. The *pisco sour* is not difficult to prepare. One cocktail requires 3 ounces of *pisco*, 1½ teaspoons very fine sugar, 1½ teaspoons fresh lemon juice, 1 tablespoon egg white, and 3 to 4 ice cubes. The egg white and sugar are combined in a cocktail shaker until the sugar is dissolved. The *pisco*, lemon juice, and ice cubes are then added. The entire mixture is shaken vigorously, nine or ten times; then the drink is poured through a strainer into a chilled cocktail glass. The *piscola* is made by combining *pisco* and Coca-Cola to taste.

Chicha is a punch made from grapes that are beginning to ferment. If the brew is allowed to ferment fully, it becomes a wine, known as *chicha cruda* (raw *chicha*). It can also be heated, thus stopping the fermentation process (*chicha cocida* or cooked *chicha*). Along with traditional wines, *chicha* is a common drink during Independence Day celebrations on September 18.

Eggnog is a traditional drink during the December holidays in the United States. Chile has something somewhat akin to it in consistency and color, but different in taste and ingredients, which is called *cola de mono* (literally, monkey's tail). It is made with milk, coffee, sugar, and *aguardiente*, a clear brandy produced in Chile.

Pisco, cola de mono, and *chicha* are popular drinks in Chile, but it is wine for which Chile has become increasingly famous. Chileans have, of course, been savoring this product of the grape for centuries, and the country's wines have long been known in the United States, but until fairly recently, only by those who are true aficionados.

Wine was undoubtedly brought to Chile by the conquistadors, who arrived in the Central Valley in the 1540s. It had long been an essential element in the celebration of the Eucharist, and thus it is not surprising that it formed a fundamental part of the cultural conquest of the continent. It is not known whether the first vines to arrive in Chile were cut from Spanish vines growing in Peru, which had been conquered almost ten years before Chile, or whether they were brought directly from Spain by the very first conquistadors, Pedro de Valdivia, founder of Santiago, and Diego de Almagro, former colleague of Francisco Pizarro, the conqueror of Peru.

What is clear is that these vines rapidly adapted to the soil and climate of the new colony, and by the beginning of the seventeenth century, Chile had become the principal exporter of wine to the rest of the colonies of the Spanish Empire. Chile had known the grape before the Conquest, of course, and natives had used it to prepare alcoholic beverages. Still, the Spanish import was not the one which would ultimately place Chile in the forefront of the viticultural map.

In the middle of the nineteenth century, some bold entrepreneurs imported into Chile some of the finest European vines, especially from France and Germany, among them the Cabernet-Sauvignon, Cot, Merlot, Pinot, Sauvignon, Riesling, Chardonnay, and Gewurztraminer. At the same time, several experienced French enologists (scientists who deal with wine and winemaking), attracted by the favorable climatic conditions and the quality of the soil in Chile, emigrated to the country and, together with native winemakers, turned viticultural production in the more promising direction afforded by the new cuttings from France and Germany.

Chile's unique, privileged location has been instrumental in the country's being recognized as a primary center in the production of quality wines. Naturally protected by its geographic isolation—the ocean on the west, the Andes on the east, the desert in the north, and the cold and inhospitable south, Chile has proven to be fairly impervious to some of the maladies that have affected grapevines in Europe. When French and California grapevines were afflicted by the phylloxera louse, which attacks the root of the grapevine, causing the leaves to fall off and eventually killing the plant, viticulturists (synonymous with "enologists") there turned to Chile to renew their vines by returning these offspring to their original soil. Since the soil and climate of Chile's wine-growing areas parallel those found in France and California, the transplanted cuttings thrived as well in their ancestors' lands as near the Pacific coast of South America. Those vines, which bore such excellent fruit in Chile, reaped equal success in the lands that, earlier, had shared their rich bounty with Chile.

The prime areas of cultivation in Chile are between the 32nd and 38th parallels of south latitude, from just north of Santiago to the area close to the city of Temuco. The climate there is Mediterranean moderate, with warm days and cold nights, and the changes of the seasons. There are valleys, and rivers that run from the Andes to the Pacific, providing an excellent setting for the growing of grapes. The entire area covers more than 500 kilometers

A large vat at the entrance to the Concha y Toro facility in Pirque, some thirty miles south of Santiago.

(more than 300 miles) from north to south, from the Maipo River to the Maule River. In the northern Maipo Valley, there are temperature variations of some 20 degrees Celsius (36 degrees Fahrenheit) between day and night in summer. The climate varies from fairly dry to humid, thus providing an excellent environment for the many varieties of grapes that go into the production of Chilean wines.

There are close to fifty established vineyards throughout the country, and many of them have become known the world over. The largest of these, Viña Concha y Toro, is involved in the production of some 20 percent of all the wines of Chile. Its main vineyard is located in Pirque, some thirty miles south of Santiago; the property was built in 1885 by Melchor de Concha y Toro. Americans easily recognize some of these wines since they are prominently displayed and sold in supermarkets and by wine retailers throughout the United States. Among the best known wines that it produces and exports are Merlots, Cabernet Sauvignons, and a combination of these two. Deep

The Concha y Toro vineyard. Roses grow at the ends of many of the rows. Growers can gauge the amount of moisture in the ground by the condition and appearance of the flowers and leaves, which are more sensitive than the vines.

within the cavelike cellars of the Concha y Toro vineyard is a wine which bears the name *Casillero del Diablo* (where the "devil has his workshop"). This name was given by the vineyard's administrator early in the nineteenth century to keep some of the workers from sampling too much of the grape. The Cabernet Sauvignon that bears this label can be easily recognized by a little devil's figure that adorns the bottle. It has been available in the United States for several years.

An interesting part of the tour of the Concha y Toro vineyard is a stroll aboveground, where the seemingly interminable rows of vines stretch almost as far as the eye can see. There is a rosebush planted at the end of many of the rows. The flowers look beautiful, but the reason for their being there is more practical than aesthetic. Those who tend the vines can easily see the condition of the soil, especially the moisture content, from the appearance of the rosebush leaves, which are sensitive to changes in the soil. If these leaves appear dry, it is an indication that the soil needs more moisture.

Besides Concha y Toro, which advertises its wines widely in the United States as well as in Chile, many other vineyards are attaining recognition. Although some quality vineyards are still too small to be able to export their production, others have the means to begin to meet the growing foreign demand that Chilean wines are creating everyday.

No more than a half-hour from the Concha y Toro complex is the Carmen Vineyard, on the lower sides of the Andes. It was founded in 1850 and is presently undergoing a remodeling, due to be completed in 2000. Fully 99 percent of its production is exported, but the remainder is appreciated in Chile. The most distinctive of its production is the Grande Vidure Cabernet, a combination of Carmere and Cabernet Sauvignon.

Santa Rita Vineyard, a close neighbor of the Carmen Vineyard, offers a wide range of prices and types, ranging from the basic 120 line to the Reserva (Reserve), Medalla Real (Royal Medallion), and Casa Real Cabernet Sauvignon (Royal House Cabernet Sauvignon). The Casa Real is among the best of the Cabernet Sauvignons.

Undurraga is a vineyard that has a long history in Chile, and although it is not as large and well known as Concha y Toro, it still has a great tradition in the country. Its characteristic squat bottle of Cabernet Sauvignon has long been recognized by wine lovers. It belongs to the family that bears its name and has two sites, both open to the public. Fundo Santa Ana (Santa Ana Estate) is a colonial villa designed by George Dubois, a creator of gardens, in the nineteenth century; located just ten minutes southwest of Santiago. A more modern installation is south of Santiago, in the Colchagua Valley. Besides visiting the tasting room, the tourist can see the grounds on horseback or in a carriage. Among Undurraga's more distinguished wines are its Chardonnay, Cabernet Sauvignon, and Merlot.

Cousiño-Macul's vineyard is located in the southeastern sector of Santiago. It offers guided tours of the tasting room, which also houses a small museum detailing the long and colorful history of the property. In the sixteenth century, the conquistadors planted vines on the site, which earlier had been an Inca settlement called Macul. The property was held by many different owners for the next three centuries, until the Cousiño family acquired it in 1856. Today, the sixth generation of Cousiños maintains a presence there. Cousiño-Macul's wines are distinctive among Chile's production because of their fruity tastes; their much sought-after Finis Terrae wines are made with a more-than-sixty-year-old Cabernet grape (combined with Merlot) and have aromas and tastes that suggest herbs, cherries, mocha, and blackberries.

Another significant producer is the Santa Carolina Vineyard. It uses grapes from various regions: the warm Maipo Valley, the more temperate Maule Valley, and the Casablanca Valley, which has recently become the most popular area for the cultivation of grapes. It offers standard wines, among them the Reserva Merlot (Merlot Reserve), with a cherrylike taste.

Among other vineyards whose wines are increasingly appearing on market are Pedro Grand, with its Merlot; Los Nogales; Los Vascos, with, among others, its Chardonnay; Carmen, with its Merlot and Chardonnay; and Caliterra, with its Cabernet Sauvignons.

Wines from these vineyards and lesser-known ones are imported into the United States and labeled with American trademarks, such as Walnut Crest, but their country of origin can still be discerned, since the valleys where they were produced are included on the front labels (Rapel, Maule, Central Valley, for example) and "Chile" is conspicuously displayed as the country of production, usually on the back of the bottles.

Chile has long made a very decent champagne produced by Champagne Alberto Valdivieso. It has been a staple in Chile for a number of years and has become available around the world.

There is one rather substantial drink, called *ulpo*, that Chileans always associate with the outdoors and which brings memories of the countryside, the olden days, and, perhaps, campfires and "roughing it." *Ulpo* is made by combining toasted wheat flour, cold water, and sugar. The two solid ingredients are carried by the backpacker or picnicker; the water, if one wishes to be authentic, can be obtained from a flowing stream. The ingredients are mixed and consumed in whatever container has been taken along.

MEALS AND MEALTIMES

Chileans share an essentially common heritage with the rest of Latin America, yet differences and similarities abide together to make for an interesting and unique melting pot. Other Latin Americans feel at home when visiting or living in Chile because the crucible is, in some ways, similar to their own. North Americans, on the other hand, are struck by customs that seem to be so different from their own. While some visitors from the North seem uncomfortable with these contrasts, others appreciate the attitudes that have created and maintained these characteristics, and gain a better understanding of the culture they are experiencing.

Chileans eat their meals at differing times and have a different attitude towards eating and drinking. Their diet tends to be considerably more eclectic than that of Americans, and mealtimes generally last longer. In very broad terms, Chileans neither live to eat nor eat to live. Although eating fulfills a natural need, it also provides a pleasurable experience, especially if the activity can be shared with others.

Desayuno (breakfast) tends to be southern European in nature, and thus differs from what North Americans or northern Europeans might be accustomed to. Standard fare for this first meal of the day is generally *café con leche*, a combination of hot milk and strong coffee, the proportions suiting individual taste. Sugar is added as desired. Toast, with jam and butter, accompanies this beverage and tops off the meal. The larger hotels serve typically American breakfasts, consisting of juice, eggs, bacon, pancakes, and the like. Supermarkets carry the typical ingredients that make up a *desayuno americano* (American breakfast) as well. The times for this first meal of the day can be similar to those in other countries, but hotels, and especially country inns, often begin to serve breakfast later than U.S. establishments do. Breakfast buffets are not a Chilean institution, although the larger hotels in major cities tend to provide them because they usually cater to non-Chilean tourists or to Chileans wanting a change of pace.

The most typical time for *almuerzo* (lunch) is after one o'clock, perhaps nearer 1:30 P.M. A generation ago, offices gave their employees up to two and a half hours for this main meal of the day, so that they could return home, have a leisurely lunch with family, and even enjoy a short nap before returning to work. The lunch hour can still be a rather long affair, even during the workweek, and employees can still enjoy a meal at a nearby restaurant and sit back, after the food has been consumed, to discuss business, politics, or even the weather. Fewer people return home for lunch today than in the past, in part due to the tremendous growth of the cities, which, with the accompanying traffic, does not allow the commute to and from home, even in the time allotted by employers.

Since dinner, or supper, the last meal of the day, comes considerably later in Chile than in the United States, Chileans traditionally enjoy a generally light, in-between meal referred to as *el té* (loosely, "tea time") or *las once(s)*, derived from the British custom of elevenses, a light meal between ten and eleven in the morning, that can resemble breakfast or be different from it. The traditional time is five o'clock, but it can be anytime between four and six, or even a little later. Spaniards have a similar meal, called *merienda*, a name that is not unknown in Chile.

Chileans invite friends or family, or hold birthday parties for their children, at this time of day. The invitation can be tendered in the following way: *Vénganse a tomar té* (Come have tea with us), although the liquid to be consumed can be tea or coffee, or perhaps a cold drink. If it is to be coffee, it is prepared in the usual manner, *café con leche*. A not uncommon way to prepare *café con leche* for this meal, especially in summer, is as *café helado* (iced coffee); ice cream is added to the mixture, which is served in a tall glass. If the beverage is to be tea, then it has to be in the British way: hot tea with milk. Iced tea is an American concoction which might be hard to find in

Chile. Lately, however, some of the larger supermarkets, perhaps catering to this decidedly American taste, have been carrying iced tea in cans or plastic bottles.

While coffee or tea is the staple beverage for this late afternoon meal, what is consumed along with it can either resemble breakfast or become much more elaborate, depending on the occasion and on whether it is purely a family affair or a social event.

Tea time can mean toasted white bread, with butter and jam, or the traditional *marraqueta*, a firmer bread that resembles French or Italian loaves. Pastries or cake can replace bread, and the total meal can be ample enough to replace supper. Restaurants open for tea time, and there are eating establishments that cater solely to the "tea" crowd. These tearooms are known for artistically designed cakes and pastries that can be enjoyed on the premises or taken home. Tea time is a cultural experience that Chileans would be loath to do without.

Supper is typically eaten at around nine o'clock but can be served even later if it is to be a social event. It resembles lunch but is usually somewhat less abundant and elaborate, especially when it involves only the immediate family. As a social event, of course, it can expand into whatever the hosts want to make of it. This last meal of the day is referred to as *la comida* (literally, the meal). The Spanish word *la cena* ("supper") is universally understood but indicates that the speaker is not Chilean. (In the central area of Spain, especially Madrid, *la comida* is lunch. So, if someone in Chile invites a non-Chilean for a meal by saying, "*Véngase a comer*," the guest will commit a faux pas by showing up for lunch but will be "in the groove" by arriving at around nine o'clock or a bit later, unless a different time has been specified by the host.)

DRINKS WITH MEALS

Many adults consume wine with their lunch, especially if time and circumstances permit it. Since Chile is known for the high quality of its wines and for their ready availability, price is not an issue, as it can be in the United States, where a single glass of wine can sometimes approximate the cost of the main entrée. Those who do not wish to imbibe can, of course, consume nonalcoholic drinks. American soft drinks are available in both diet and regular versions. Those that have sugar in them tend to be somewhat sweeter than their counterparts in the United States. For this reason, those who wish to have a drink that is not as sweet will sometimes use a slice of lemon to counter the heavier infusion of sugar. Chile has nationally produced soft drinks as well. Beer, both domestic and imported, is widely available. Tap water is completely safe in Chile, and is commonly served with lunch and supper.

Coffee is not normally served with lunch or supper, but is enjoyed at the end of the meal. Both eating establishments and private homes usually serve instant coffee rather than the percolated or drip variety. And this is done quite openly: the coffee is brought in still in the can, with the manufacturer plainly shown on the container. If one wishes to have an espresso, one needs to ask for a *cafecito* (literally, a "little coffee"); then one will be served excellent "real" coffee.

Chileans enjoy mineral water, both carbonated (*con gas*) and still (*sin gas*). It is commonly consumed, especially by those who do not wish to drink wine or beer with their meal. There are many brands, and they tend to be rather uniform in taste and in the amount of carbonation (for those that are *con gas*). On one occasion, a waiter was heard to say, when asked about the innate differences between brands, that they were "all from the same tap." Panimávida and Cachantún are brands that have been on the market for many years. In general, mineral water resembles club soda quite closely except that the carbon dioxide content is much lower.

THE CHILEAN CONCEPT OF TIME

Time, of course, is a relative concept, as most non–Latin Americans have long suspected, at least when it comes to social events. Thus, if an invitation is tendered for lunch, tea, or supper, the guest(s) would do well to arrive at least a few minutes late. If the event is a party, then it's "no-holds-barred." Americans not accustomed to being "fashionably late," are generally the only ones to be punctual or to arrive early, and many have been embarrassed when they realize that their hosts are not ready for their arrival. Chileans are not unaware of American punctuality, and are sure to be understanding even if they are unprepared for the early arrivals.

The same cannot be said for work and school hours, as well as train, bus, and airplane schedules, which tend to be geared to punctuality. Still, the traveler should not be completely surprised if opening times, especially, are not always strictly adhered to, even if there has been a gradual, albeit grudging, move toward observing the demands of contemporary life.

Finally, it is worthwhile noting that Chileans, like other Latin Americans and Spaniards, like to enjoy a leisurely meal, whenever this is possible, where food is consumed in the company of good friends or family, and where time enjoyed after the meal is over (*la sobremesa*, sitting at the table after the meal) is an important experience. It is one cultural tradition that Chileans would be loath to abandon even if it seems to clash with the pace of modern life.

SPORTS

Soccer

Like most of its South American neighbors and many of the countries in the world, Chile shares a passion for soccer, known by its Spanish name, *fútbol*, at every level. There are professional teams, some associated with the universities and others with specific ethnic entities. Two traditional rivals are the Universidad de Chile (University of Chile) and the Universidad Católica (Catholic University). One team that bears a historical name taken from an Araucanian hero featured in Ercilla's *La Araucana* is Colo Colo, one of the perennially strong teams in the nation.

Although Chile does not rank among the traditionally strong soccer nations of opLatin America, such as Argentina, Brazil, and Uruguay, it did host the World Cup in 1962, and performed quite admirably. Some of its players have joined European teams, but when the World Cup comes, every four years, these players return to play for their country of birth. Such was the case with two of Chile's top players, Iván Zamorano and Marcelo Salas, who play for non-Chilean teams. In 1998, they both played for Chile in the World Cup.

Children often begin playing soccer at a young age, sometimes as soon as they are able to walk. It is not uncommon to see entire families playing in their backyards, from three- or four-year-olds to sixty-plus grandparents.

Tennis

Chile has produced world-class tennis players. Hans Gildemeister and Patricio Fillol have been ranked among the top players in the world in years past, and Marcelo Ríos obtained the number one ranking in the world for a short period early in 1999, making Chileans proud of him.

Skiing

Just when European and North American skiers hang up their skis in the early spring, Chileans begin to prepare their equipment for Chile's ski season, which begins in May and runs through November, depending on the ski resort. There are excellent sites from the Central Valley, where Santiago is located, to the extreme south, near Punta Arenas.

Three generations of a Chilean family enjoy a backyard soccer game, a common pastime on weekends or during holidays.

Chile's most famous resort is Portillo, located approximately 90 miles east of Santiago, at an altitude of 9,450 feet above sea level. Skiing season there runs from the middle of June until the middle of October. The accommodations are relatively expensive since the resort attracts mostly well-to-do skiers.

Much closer than Portillo, almost within sight of the capital, are several other ski centers, some only 50 kilometers (31 miles) from Santiago. Valle Nevado (Snowy Valley) is some 60 kilometers (38 miles) east of the capital; this site and La Parva (meaning "small"), El Colorado (The Red One), and Farellones (literally, "rocky outcrops"), which are 10 kilometers (6 miles) closer to Santiago, comprise the largest ski area in the southern hemisphere. On clear days, skiers can see the metropolitan area of Santiago from Farellones. Skiers ranging from beginners to experts can find excellent slopes and lodging facilities. Since these areas are nearer Santiago and at lower altitudes than Portillo, the skiing season goes from the middle of June until the end of September.

There are other excellent skiing areas all along the Andes from the Central

Valley to almost the tip of the continent, some of these near the lake region and abutting similar areas across the border in Argentina. The skiing areas south of the Central Valley tend to be at lower altitudes, between 1,000 and 2,000 meters (3,300 to 6,600 feet), but the season is as long as it is east of Santiago, if not a bit longer, due to their more southerly location.

Equestrian Sports

Chile has long been known for breeding fine horses. The Chilean rodeo, different from its counterpart in the United States, relies on the strength and dexterity developed in these animals, specifically to participate in this demanding and artistic sport. Horse and rider must pin the running bull against the wall of the enclosure, gently but precisely. There are haciendas devoted to the breeding of these fine horses much as fine fighting bulls are raised in Spain's Andalusia.

But Chile has long raised horses for purposes other than the rodeo. The Hipódromo (Santiago racetrack) is the center for equestrian sports where professional riders exhibit their skills and their horses which have been specifically bred to participate in exhibitions of fine horsemanship. The Carabineros, Chile's police force, have long maintained a tradition of participation in equestrian exhibitions that reflect their original status as mounted troops. Some of the nation's finest riders still come from their ranks, and many have gone on to participate in exhibitions both at home and abroad.

SOCIAL CUSTOMS

Personal Distance

Americans who travel abroad quickly become aware that nationals of other countries do not appear to be concerned with maintaining a certain distance between themselves and others. This is obvious, for example, when one travels in public conveyances or when people stand in line before entering museums, post offices, or banks. Contact is often made between total strangers who seem unaware that they have bumped against someone else as they go about their business.

Chileans exhibit this same unconcern when they find themselves in crowds. Commuters using public transportation, such as city buses or the Santiago metro, often find themselves closely pressed, one against the other, during the rush hour. In contrast, New York subway riders, or Chicago commuters taking the El, who even in crowded cars, try to maintain some breathing room among themselves.

What happens in public with complete strangers also takes place among acquaintances, friends, and families. It begins with introductions. Americans, who are accustomed to maintaining a certain distance between themselves and even friends and family, often remark that at first they feel uncomfortable when Europeans or Latin Americans place themselves closer to them than they expect. It is not uncommon for those from the United States to edge away slightly from Chileans with whom they are conversing as the latter, unaware of the others' discomfort, close the gap once again.

Greetings

Chileans almost always shake hands when introduced: men shake hands with men; women shake hands with women; and men and women shake hands with each other. On subsequent occasions, men who have been previously introduced again shake hands, and will continue to do so whenever they see each other. The custom with women, and with men and women, can vary. If women maintain a formal relationship with other women, they may continue to shake hands after they have been introduced. If the relationship is less formal, it is very common for two women to hold hands loosely as each plants a perfunctory kiss on the other's cheek. When men and women meet again, in a formal situation hands are shaken. If the second meeting is social, it is very common for a woman and a man to act as two women will: holding hands loosely, each kisses the other lightly on the cheek. But, in contrast with the custom in Spain, for example, there is only a kiss on one cheek and not one on both cheeks. Males who are introduced to their sisters' or mothers' female friends in a social situation will usually kiss them on the cheek; they shake other males' hands.

Members of a family, whether nuclear or extended, greet one another with a kiss on the cheek after a brief separation of even one day. Good-byes are extended in the same manner. Males, unless they are very young, shake hands with relatives of the same gender. Sometimes, brothers or fathers and sons who have been apart for a considerable amount of time will clasp one another in a loose embrace (the *abrazo*), often shaking hands at the same time.

Clearly, greetings, whether in formal, social, or family situations, can take up a considerable amount of time. Americans, accustomed to entering an acquaintance's home and simply nodding to the people assembled in a room, may be surprised to see others coming in and circulating throughout a room as they shake hands or kiss all who are there. Soon, however, they begin to realize that Chileans value intimacy and that physical contact, whether a handshake, a kiss on the cheek, or a loose hug, is an important demonstration of their appreciation of those with whom they interact. Chilean women, like other Latin American and many European females, link arms when walking along the street, especially if they are members of the same family.

Americans, especially those who live in small communities, often greet perfect strangers as they pass in the street, in the supermarket, in church, or anyplace where people are bound to congregate. Chileans, on the other hand, at times appear to be unaware that there are others around them. To Chileans, Americans may appear to be too "chummy" with strangers; to Americans, Chileans may seem to be standoffish.

At the same time, the often-heard expression "Mi casa es tu casa" (My house is your house) or "Estás en tu casa" (You are in your own home), said by Chileans to someone who has entered their home, tends to be tendered in a more heartfelt manner than an American southerner's "Y'all come see me, now." Americans, then, appear to be more open, within limits, even with strangers; Chileans, on the other hand, will almost literally offer you their very homes once a certain link has been established.

The Saint's Day

The celebration of one's saint's day is religious in origin, and the practice has existed since the days of the early Church. Every day of the year usually commemorates a saint or two. In the past, some predominantly Roman Catholic countries have not permitted their citizens to use any names for their children that are not found in the officially sanctioned calendar. Some well-known saints' days are those of San Juan Bautista (St. John the Baptist) on June 24, San Guillermo (St. William) on June 25, San Ignacio de Loyola (St. Ignatius of Loyola) on July 31, San Patricio (St. Patrick) on March 17, Santa Sara (St. Sarah) on October 22, and San Andrés (St. Andrew) on November 30.

Parents sometimes elect to honor the saints on whose day their children are born. Thus, March 17 often sees a number of children named for the patron saint of Ireland. Most fathers and mothers, however, select their own names, and they and their offspring honor the saint whose name their child bears on the specified day. Savvy children often expect presents on both their birthdays and their saints' days (preferably different days of the year). There are probably some children who, taking advantage of the fact that they possess two given names, attempt to remind generous adults of their saints' days (in the plural).

Adults who choose to suffer amnesia when their birthdays roll around are often pleased to accept congratulations on their saint's day. Even though their saint's day comes once a year, the fact that it does not commemorate the passing of time lessens the chance that some inquisitive soul will allude to the number of years being celebrated. The common congratulatory expression on the saint's day is *Feliz Santo* (Happy Saint's Day) or, more specifically, *Feliz San Patricio* (Happy St. Patrick's Day) to their friends born on March 17.

Stores often place advertisements on their display windows reminding passersby of the particular saint who is being honored on that particular day. On July 31 then, shoppers can purchase cards, chocolates, or flowers in honor of friends or family who bear the name of the Spanish founder of the Society of Jesus (the Jesuits). Women can choose the feminine version of the name of a male saint. Thus, a woman whose name is Juana (Joan) can celebrate on June 24, even though there is a day that commemorates Santa Juana de Arco (St. Joan of Arc).

Although the religious origin of the saint's day celebration is remembered and honored, many Chileans who are not religious commemorate the feast day and offer their congratulations to family or friends who bear the particular name of the day. It is very common for children to be reminded of their grandparents' saints' days so that appropriate congratulations, letters, cards, or homemade gifts can be offered to their parents' parents. Children who are Roman Catholics have godparents whose names are sometimes bestowed on them, as the godchildren. Those godparents (*padrino* and *madrina*) are honored on their respective saints' days.

Forms of Address

Those who have studied Spanish learned early on that Spanish speakers have two ways of addressing one another, whereas modern English has only one (you). When speaking to a child or a close friend or family member, the Spanish speaker uses the familiar form, *tú* (in older English, "thou"), and when addressing someone more formally, *usted* is used. Both forms mean "you" in English, but the native speaker knows not to use both with one individual. If the relationship changes and becomes less formal, some signal is usually given that makes both individuals comfortable enough to switch from *usted* to *tú*.

Chileans have a unique usage of these two forms of address, however. When a young man and a young woman meet socially, *tú* is almost always chosen as the form of address. However, if and when the relationship progresses from being a purely social one to one that is more intimate and exclusive, both male and female switch from *tú* to *usted*, and continue to do so for as long as the relationship continues. Many have remarked that they have been unaware of the exact moment when this takes place. Even when the relationship leads to marriage, husbands and wives retain this special, intimate use of *usted*, not because they have become more formal, but because it signals a new form of respect that identifies the special relationship. Sometimes this special use of *usted* is employed by parents when addressing their children; the latter, in turn, use it with their parents. And there is another special usage of *usted*, when parents are addressing children who refuse to obey. When children hear the switch from *tú* to *usted*, they quickly become aware that a parent is out of patience. English-speaking parents do something similar to this when they switch from a simple first name or nickname to addressing their children by their full names.

The "Uniform" and Other Clothing

Chilean men tend to be conservative in the way they dress, although this has been changing slightly. There has always been a joke, which is perhaps not far from the truth, that men tend to wear anything they wish, as long as their pants are gray and their jackets are blue, or the other way around. Women, on the other hand, can dress however they wish.

When the weather turns cool, it is common to see men in the traditional "uniform" described above, with a sweater under the jacket, and a scarf around the neck to ward off the chill. On rare occasions, they don an overcoat, but it often comes off later in the day as temperatures climb into the upper fifties or low sixties (Fahrenheit).

Women have never been as conservative as men in the clothing that they wear, although bright colors are generally eschewed. On more than one occasion, male tourists have stood out from the crowd, not because of their physical appearance but due to their clothing. There are many chuckles when Chileans see an American who has traveled to Chile on business, dressed in a lightweight tropical suit, disembarking from his plane at Pudahuel Airport, only to face the southern winter.

Women's Roles

Chile's largely Hispanic inheritance would seem to indicate that women are relegated to their traditional role in the more conservative societies. In many ways, this has been the case throughout much of the nation's history, but there have been, and there continue to be, many exceptions to this perception that women are subservient to men in Chilean society.

Women did not achieve the right to vote until 1949, almost three decades after this happened in the United States. Until as recently as the early 1970s, married women were not allowed to leave the country without their spouses' permission. Many changes have occurred in recent years, however, and women and men stand much more equally before the law.

In spite of these and many other imbalances in men's and women's roles, women have been able to receive an education and join professions for many years. Aside from the traditional role of women as teachers, they have also entered medicine and the law. The nation's Congress has many female members, and there was one woman candidate for president in the elections of December 1999.

There is an interesting corollary to women's changing roles in society, especially with regard to their entrance into more and more of the traditionally masculine professions. The language is undergoing changes to accommodate this growing presence of women in the ranks of professions which, until recently, were largely, if not completely, occupied by men.

The word *arquitecto* (architect) existed only in the masculine form (ending in the letter *o*). Even when a woman entered the field of architecture, she would be identified as an *arquitecto*. Likewise, an attorney would be referred to as an *abogado*, regardless of sex. In the more distant past, the wife of a professional or an important politician was referred to by her husband's title with the feminine ending of *a*, to signify that she was the wife of that male individual.

Today, a growing number of professional women identify themselves as *arquitectas* or *abogadas*, the *as* ending indicating that they are women. Even the term *médico*, which in Spanish is the most common word for "physician," has come to be used in the feminine when it refers to women, even though in the past, and in many societies even in the present, the term *médica* has sometimes connoted a healer who does not possess a medical degree.

Chilean society still does not legally approved of divorce, although it has been the subject of heated and controversial study. Legal separation has existed for a long time, but since it does not dissolve a marriage, it effectively prohibits the remarriage of either spouse. The argument over divorce does not solely pit men against women; it is supported or rejected by many on both sides of the issue.

Women's more traditional role as homemakers—mother, cook, and dishwasher—have slowly been undergoing changes, some subtle, others more rapid. Whereas just a few years ago, no man would have been caught in the kitchen, helping to cook or wash, many have now taken on the role of helpers to their wives.

The battle for equality in the home and in the workplace is an ongoing process, however. It is often the case, for example, that ads for employment state that females applying for a position should be between the ages of eighteen and thirty-five, for example, and that a photograph must be appended to the application. The same is not usually asked of male applicants, and when it is, the upper age limit is often several years higher. It is only a matter of time before workplace discrimination in age and appearance is effectively challenged by both men and women.

4

Broadcasting and Print Media

MAJOR NEWSPAPERS

THE FIRST NEWSPAPER in Chile was the *Aurora de Chile*, the first issue of which appeared on February 13, 1812. The name is apt, since *aurora* means "dawn." It was not, to say the least, a publication which purported to be impartial, since its editorial perspective was decidedly pro-patriot and anti-Spanish. Still, it did signal to the budding independence movement that the nation was, indeed, being born, and that news coverage was of importance to those who saw Chile as a distinct national entity. Its publisher was Fray Camilo Henríquez, who had been born in the southern city of Valdivia in 1769. While a student in Lima, he had suffered persecution at the hands of the Inquisition, for reading and propagating the philosophical ideas of the French Enlightenment and, as a result, was almost expelled from the religious order to which he belonged. When he became aware that a revolution for independence had broken out in Chile, Henríquez returned to his land of birth in January 1811, and promoted the break with Spain vociferously, publishing his views under the name Quirino Lemáchez, and anagram of his real name. Impressed by his oratory and dedication, José Miguel Carrera named him the editor of *La Aurora*, which rapidly became the budding government's national voice.

La Aurora, which appeared weekly on Thursdays, consisted of a single sheet. Many of Chile's patriots collaborated in its publication, among them Antonio José de Irisarri; Juan Egaña; Manuel de Salas, first director of the National Library and promoter of the abolition of slavery; José Miguel Infante, a legislator who, with Salas, was instrumental in the enactment of the emancipation laws of 1811 and 1823; and Manuel José Gandarillas. This first newspaper had a life of only some fourteen months, ending publication on April 1, 1813. *El Monitor Araucano*, also edited by Henríquez, succeeded *La Aurora*.

El Mercurio de Valparaíso (The Mercury of Valparaiso) was founded in that city on September 12, 1827. Now in its 173rd consecutive year of existence, this "messenger" of the day's news is considered to be the oldest, continuously published newspaper in the Spanish language. Its first issue consisted of four pages with a potpourri of news items of general interest to the population of Valparaíso, and its subtitle, *Periódico Mercantil y Político* (Political and Mercantile Newspaper) indicated the publication's purpose. Aside from reporting some of the significant events of the day, it also contained letters addressed to the editorial staff, a list of those in the hospital and the jails, and weather conditions at 9 A.M. on the day of its publication. There was also general information on the port's activities for the day, including ship arrivals and departures for the Peruvian port of Callao, which serves Lima. Like many other newspapers, *El Mercurio de Valparaíso* today has a web page: www.mercuriovalp.cl.

Although still a significant newspaper, *El Mercurio* is no longer as well known as Santiago's *El Mercurio*, which was at first the capital's version of the original in Valparaíso, but today is an independent newspaper. It was founded in Santiago on June 1, 1900. Although separate from its older progenitor, it still acknowledges its provenance on the cover page.

Like most major newspapers, *El Mercurio* appears seven days a week, with the daily version having some fifty pages and the Sunday publication being considerably larger. All editions contain national and international news, and the general presentation is sober, serious, and correct. Some see its presentation as conservative; others, as impartial. During the Allende presidency (1970–1973), the editorial stance was decidedly in opposition to those policies which the staff saw as destabilizing and undemocratic. During the early 1970s, Chile's largest paper mill, Papeles y Cartones (Paper and Cardboard), was threatened by a takeover from the socialist government. *El Mercurio* feared that its opposition would be stifled by government control of the supply of newsprint. During the Pinochet dictatorship, *El Mercurio*, in the eyes of many in the opposition, practiced what might be referred to as measured self-censorship, exhibiting criticism in a manner that it deemed judicious and nondeclamatory. Whatever its political or social inclinations at present, the newspaper is clearly at the forefront of the press in Chile, and it continues to be the yardstick by which quality journalism is measured.

The Sunday edition contains heavy advertising (as do the six daily issues) and includes several supplements, among them a literary review, a weekend magazine, and a television guide for the week. The financial pages are inclusive and reflect Chile's growing membership in the world business community. *El Mercurio*'s web page (www.elmercurio.cl) contains the latest headlines and some of the supplements available in the hard copy of the paper.

La Segunda, La Tercera, El Diario, La Nación (until 1990, perceived to be the voice of the government), and *La Hora* are other newspapers that appear in Santiago. Chile's other large cities have publications of their own, and their papers circulate regionally.

Concepción, 300 miles south of the capital, has a long-lived newspaper, *El Sur*. Founded on November 15, 1882, the first edition of *El Sur* had only four pages. Two nearby ports, Talcahuano and Coronel, gave this newest contribution to journalism a strong niche in the nation's press. At the time of its first appearance, the War of the Pacific was ending and the government of President Domingo Santa María was bringing to an end the long struggles between nonindigenous Chileans and the indomitable Araucanians, most of whom lived in the area from Concepción south. During the Civil War of 1891, *El Sur* denounced what it perceived to be the dictatorship of President José Manuel Balmaceda. It supported reform of the Constitution of 1833, and individual liberty. It promoted secular primary education, free and available to all, and asked for the separation of Church and state, a concept that became reality in 1925. Due to its editorial rejection of the executive's policies, the paper was prevented from publishing between January and August 1891. When the forces of Congress defeated the president's troops, *El Sur* resumed publication.

The German colony, centered in the area of Valdivia, has had access to newspapers in its own language since 1870, when the first German-language publication, *Deutsche Nachrichten* (German Press), made its debut in Valparaíso. Some twenty-five newspapers in that language have appeared since then in several areas of Chile, particularly where Germans have settled. *El Cóndor*, first published in 1938, was the fusion of three other German-language papers. *El Cóndor* appears every Friday. It publishes Chilean, German, and generally European news, items of cultural interest, business articles, and interviews. In June 1998, *El Cóndor* celebrated its sixtieth year of uninterrupted publication. Even though the paper includes news from Europe in general, and from Germany in particular, most articles concern domestic matters of interest to the German-Chilean community. Its weekly circulation is 6,000 copies; the newspaper estimates that between 15,000 and

20,000 have access to each issue. *El Cóndor* is also sold in Germany, Switzerland, Austria, Belgium, the United States, and some Latin American countries.

Santiago also has English-language newspapers. The *Santiago Times* is a daily newspaper that provides national, business, and mining news. Its classified pages are free. *Business News America* is dedicated to providing news of the business world. Another business newspaper that has been appearing since 1978 is *Estrategia*. Its web page still looks somewhat amateurish, but it purports to be the first Latin American publication to have created one. These two publications and many others have web pages.

In metropolitan areas such as Santiago, Valparaíso, and Viña del Mar, some of the more recognized papers from around the world, such as the *New York Times*, the *Washington Post*, the *Los Angeles Times*, the *Times* of London, and *El País* of Madrid, are available.

MAGAZINES

Magazines are available in Chile, in Spanish and English, the latter published both in the country and abroad. Some of these have been available for years; others are new.

Perhaps the best known of the domestic magazines is *Ercilla*, a publication that covers the news for a fourteen-day period, from Sunday to Sunday. It resembles American publications such as *Time* and *Newsweek*, with a potpourri of offerings ranging from news to items of cultural interest. Among its sections are editorial pages, domestic and international news, social events, restaurant recommendations, and literary news with reviews of recent publications and interviews of writers. Its movie section features the latest films, with reviews, ratings, and box office success. Readers' mail, Internet news, television offerings, and a crossword puzzle round out the magazine. Those interested in accessing the latest issue can do so by using its web page (www.ercilla.cl).

This publication bears the name of the young Spanish captain who wrote Chile's and America's first epic poem in the Spanish language (*La Araucana*), written in the middle of the sixteenth century and published some twenty years later in Spain. *Ercilla's* creators knew well that its association with that illustrious poet would greatly aid readers' recognition.

Ercilla's political stance was considered conservative until the early months of the 1973 coup d'état. Shortly after that event, the magazine published graphic photographs of the bombed Moneda Palace; the arms cache reportedly in Salvador Allende's Tomás Moro residence, one of several homes owned by the former executive; and several reports which appeared to give the armed forces' perspective on the military takeover of the government.

Qué Pasa ("What's Happening") is a weekly magazine that stresses hard news and opinion more than *Ercilla*. A recent issue featured election news, the memoirs of Henry Kissinger, and the clashes between the government and the Mapuche Indians, who have become activists in their quest for protection against pressures exerted by the lumber industry.

Whereas *Ercilla* might be considered a middle-of-the-road publication, comfortably ensconced in a niche that "rocks not the boat," *Qué Pasa*, whose title seems to strike a more confrontational stance, attracts the reading public by intimating that it might be delving beyond appearances to find the "real" news, what's happening beyond the obvious. The relative newness of this magazine makes it avant-garde compared to the sedate and well-established *Ercilla*, which some consider staid. Although their formats are similar with full-color front covers and color throughout the inside pages, *Ercilla* appears to invest more of its resources on paper and photographic quality. *Qué Pasa* can be accessed at www.quepasa.cl.

Another relatively recent arrival in the world of magazines is *Cosas* (Things), first published in 1976, which appears weekly and advertises itself as "Una Revista Internacional" (an international magazine). It resembles many of the publications that readers can find at almost any newsstand. Its format is similar to that of well-established magazines such as *Elle*, and it has something of that publication, with a smidgen of *People* and others in that niche, although its attractive colors and size give it a more serious appearance.

The magazine's international focus is accentuated by its attention to a wide coverage of news, and features that go well beyond the Chilean scene. Although there is political news, domestic and international, a great number of its articles could be considered "everyday living" features, including both the weighty (articles on drug addiction and its consequences) and the "fluff" (Michael Jackson, Prince William, et al.); thus, something for everyone. Its graphics are appealing, and the magazine's cost (more than $5 per issue) reflects the fact that its readership is select. The magazine's full-page advertisers for high-end products, such as expensive perfumes and elegant couturiers, are another indication of the intended market. Those who are interested can peruse *Cosas* at www.cosas.com.

A magazine with a very similar name but with a different readership is *Casas* (Homes). It bears a striking resemblance to American publications such as *Southern Living* and *Good Housekeeping*, although it appears biweekly and is quite slim. It is not sold, but appears as an insert included with *Cosas*. It provides consumers with information about housing, most of it high end, and with spectacular furnishings that those on the high end of the economic ladder might want to place in their beautiful homes and apartments.

Interspersed among offerings of homes and furniture are references to the in-crowd and recent social events. An interesting segment of the magazine is a real estate section, which advertises the sale of some of Santiago's plushest residences. The magazine's format would seem to make it an eclectic publication, combining light news and commercial advertising, directed at a relatively small segment of the public. Both *Cosas* and *Casas* reflect Chile's growing free-market economy, for consumerism is one of the words that define the country as the twenty-first century begins.

Chile's *Sports Illustrated* is *El Gráfico* (The Graphic), which features sports figures from Chile and the world. Since it seeks to promote the domestic scene, it more often than not features stories related to Chile's soccer (*fútbol*) stars, both those who play on professional teams in the country and those select few who play for international teams or join the national team for the World Cup. As might be expected, Chile's high-ranked tennis player Marcelo Ríos (popularly known as "el Chino"), is frequently featured in the magazine, and will continue to be as long as he remains among the world's top players. Internationally known figures are not omitted, however; a recent issue provides a nostalgic view of Muhammad Ali, a boxer who has grown beyond his reputation of thirty years ago.

Condorito (Little Condor) is the quintessential Chilean magazine. A biweekly pictorial publication, *Condorito* has been a fixture on Chilean newsstands since 1945. The Andean condor is to Chile what the eagle is to Mexico and the United States. It appears on the Chilean coat of arms along with the *huemul*, a deerlike animal native to the country; it stands for Chile's tenacity and dedication to independence and freedom. Thus, this largest of all vultures has always been identified with the nation and with its spirit. It is only logical, then, that the creator of *Condorito*, René Ríos Boettiger, also known as Pepo, would choose this majestic bird of the high Andes as the symbol of his publication.

Condorito has human traits, much like Walt Disney's Mickey Mouse, Donald Duck, and Goofy. Most of the other characters with whom he interacts are human except for the domestic pets that, like Pluto in Disney's classics, maintain their animal traits. Beyond his avian head and beak, Condorito is all human, with the strengths and weaknesses of any *Homo sapien*. Condorito can be a bum, a salesman, a policeman, a physician—in short, he can assume any role or profession that exists in Chile. For that matter, he can be a classical Roman, a visiting tourist, or even a typical Mexican *charro* (cowboy), but he never loses the persona that identifies him with the very essence of what a Chilean is.

Condorito has a nephew who lives with him. Condy is an exact replica of his uncle except for his size and naïveté. Condorito's great love is Yayita, today liberated from her limited role in the early years of the magazine's publication. Yayita lives with her parents, the imposing Mrs. Tremebunda (literally "fearful" or "terrifying") and Mr. Cuasimodo, a quiet, unassuming man who sometimes sides with his potential son-in-law against the diatribes of his domineering spouse. Yayita has a niece named Kiwi who is her aunt in miniature, exhibiting all of the characteristic innocence of childhood and the joys that are an essential part of it. Rounding out the cast is Yayita's other suitor, Pepe Cortisona, who is long on ego and short on intellect. The entire cast of *Condorito* is described, in both Spanish and English, on the magazine's web page, www.condorito.cl.

The enduring value of *Condorito*, now in its second fifty years of existence, lies in the way its creator can depict Chilean reality at an apparently comedic level, in much the same way that *All in the Family* and *I Love Lucy* did in U.S. television from the 1950s through the 1970s. The picaresque nature of Condorito also presents a parallel with another quintessential Chilean type, the *roto* (described elsewhere in this book), and this further endears the character to Chileans who, even though critical of the avian hero's foibles, still appreciate the humanity of this bird who so resembles them in the best and worse times.

There are business-oriented publications, available both in Spanish and English, which reach beyond Chile's borders. Among these are the monthly *Latin Trade*, a part of *Business Week*, and *Business News Americas*. Given Chile's growing presence in the world of business and international trade, such publications are becoming increasingly significant to those within and outside of the country.

Newsmagazines such as the U.S. *Time* and *Newsweek*, and the Germany *Der Spiegel*, are also available, especially in the larger metropolitan areas. These are often international editions which attempt to include news items tailored to the interests of communities outside the United States. More and more, some of these non-Chilean publications are beginning to appear in Spanish editions.

RADIO

Radio in Chile dates back to the 1920s. Until the advent of television some forty years ago, radio was the most important of the broadcast media, and stations, both AM and FM, came into existence shortly after their advent elsewhere. Since FM provides a much better quality of reception, it has the most prestige among listeners.

Radio El Conquistador (93.3 FM) was Chile's first station to broadcast exclusively in FM, beginning in 1963. The following year, the station was the first to add stereophonic sound. Several technological advances followed, among them quadraphonic sound, full logic stereo, and high definition (HD) FM. It has eighteen stations, located in most of Chile's main cities. Its programming includes music that appeals to a varied listening public of all economic strata and ages: Chilean folk music, classical music, popular music. The station's directorship unabashedly claims that Radio Conquistador would have pleased the medium's creator, Guglielmo Marconi.

Decidedly highbrow is Radio Beethoven (96.5 FM), in existence for many decades. It broadcasts exclusively classical music, as its name would indicate; those who are familiar with New York's WQXR would find many similarities between these two stations.

In 1959, Radio Usach (94.5 FM and 124 AM) began its transmissions as Radio Universidad Técnica del Estado (State Technical University Radio). Today the acronym Usach stands for Universidad de Santiago de Chile (University of Santiago de Chile). It is the oldest station in Chile whose mission is to transmit and diffuse academic, artistic, and cultural programs. Radio Zero (97.7 FM) has the stated aim to bridge and unite different generations of listeners. Whether its goal is achievable remains to be seen, since it believes that parents and children can equally enjoy and appreciate performers such as Bob Dylan, the Rolling Stones, and The Doors.

Among the many other radio stations vying for the attention of the listening public are Uradio, a rock station; Radio Manquehue, which advertises itself as an adult rock station; and several others, on both the AM and FM dials.

TELEVISION

Television arrived in Chile in 1959. Until the early 1970s, it was available only in the Central Valley, principally in Santiago. In July 1969, all flights and buses traveling to the capital from as far south as Puerto Montt were booked solid with space enthusiasts trying to reach Santiago before the twentieth of the month so as to be able to view the Apollo 9 landing on the moon. Today, of course, television is found nationwide.

Televisión Nacional de Chile (Chilean National Television) is a public channel, independent of the government, that advertises its primary mission as informing, educating, and entertaining the public. It was the first to have a national network (1968), color (1978), satellite transmission (1986), international transmission (1986), and stereo sound (1993).

Aside from the domestic channels, Chileans can enjoy cable, which gives them access to most of the other television providers worldwide. CNN can be accessed in both English and Spanish, as can transmission of television in German, Italian, and other languages. The ever-present *telenovelas* (soaps) are available as well. Some of these *telenovelas* are domestic; many are produced in Mexico and Brazil.

5

Literature

MUCH OF WHAT IS KNOWN about the conquest of the New World has been recorded in the chronicles written by the Conquistadors themselves. Thus, for example, the world has written records of Columbus's first voyage to the New World in 1492, and of Hernán Cortés's conquest of the Aztec Empire, beginning in 1519. Chile, fortuitously, had an epic poem written as well of the Conquistadors who participated in the struggle to conquer the new nation.

The period between this early chronicle in the late 1500s and the advent of Chilean independence from Spain in the early 1800s is not significant, however, and it is not until the neoclassic period, that begins after Chilean independence from Spain, that the nation begins to establish itself in the realm of literature.

Successive works, from the early nineteenth century through the present, mirror the literary trends in existence throughout Europe and the United States. The Romantic and Realist periods produce works that, employing the techniques of those movements, depict and describe the development of Chile as a nation and as a society. One major novelist chronicles a significant portion of the entire nineteenth century, depicting life in Chile during its successful struggle for independence from Spain, the emergence of the country's middle class, and the lives of members of the aristocracy who are intent finding their role in the new nation. A short story writer wrote pieces that raised the consciousness of Chilean society, making it aware of the struggles of workers in the nation's mines during the early 1900s.

The twentieth century produced two Nobel Prize–winning poets who, along with others who wrote in that genre, helped to make many critics refer to Chile as a "nation of poets." But the second half of this same century saw the emergence of many significant novelists, some of them members of the "Boom" in Latin American literature that existed during much of the third quarter of the 1900s. One of the novelists heavily influenced by the "Boom" is widely recognized today as, perhaps, the major writer publishing in Spanish as the twenty-first century begins.

ALONSO DE ERCILLA Y ZÚÑIGA

It is seldom the case that a nation's first work of literature is composed during the time of the nation's creation. Alonso de Ercilla y Zúñiga brandished the sword in one hand and the pen in the other, for while a member of the Spanish forces sent to Chile from Peru to conquer the seemingly indomitable Araucanians, the soldier/poet penned the more than 3,000 verses of the continent's first epic poem even as each day's sounds of battle were still echoing in the Central Valley of Chile.

Ercilla was born in Madrid in 1533. A year later his father died, but fortunately his mother obtained a post as lady-in-waiting for Empress Isabel, wife of Charles V. This allowed her to take the child to the palace on numerous occasions, thus opening important doors for him. The lad became close to Charles's son, Philip, and accompanied the heir to the throne on his travels to Italy, Germany, Austria, Flanders, and France. At the age of twenty-one, Alonso accompanied Philip to England, preparatory to the prince's wedding to Mary Tudor.

Alonso left England and traveled to Chile. It is believed that a combination of events led him to make the decision to leave a promising future in the English court. Pedro de Valdivia, founder of Santiago and Chile's first governor, had been defeated and killed by the Araucanians. A love affair gone sour and a keen interest in the events that were transpiring in Chile added to the mix, and Ercilla asked Philip for permission to return to Spain, where he obtained the license to travel to Peru.

In Lima, García Hurtado de Mendoza, son of the viceroy of Peru, was preparing an expeditionary force that was to travel south to Chile to engage the Araucanians, who were flush with their victory over Valdivia. Ercilla joined the force as a captain, and at the age of twenty-three, accompanied don García.

Ercilla remained in Chile for only three years (1556–1559), then returned to Lima and subsequently moved back to Spain, where he remained until his death in 1594, at the age of sixty-two. Several events contributed to his brief sojourn in America, not least of which was the enmity that grew between him and don García. Nevertheless, those few years in Chile were enough to mark him as one of the greatest poets of the new continent and of the late Renaissance in Spain. He had begun as a soldier, but it was his pen that would immortalize him, both in literature and in Chilean history.

La Araucana is a work deserving praise as much for its literary merit as for its value as a significant chronicle detailing the birth of the new nation. It is clear, from a reading of the poem, that Ercilla described his adversaries in a style that exhibited his Renaissance education. Chileans today feel that the poem's protagonists, among them Caupolicán and Colo Colo, are so clearly depicted that it is almost as if they had been photographed. More distinctive, however, is Ercilla's impartiality in his depiction of the two armies. Some critics believe that don García's enmity toward Alonso might have been due, at least to some degree, to the Spanish commander's perception that the poet was often more lavish in his praise of the indigenous inhabitants than he was of the soldiers of the expeditionary force sent to conquer them.

Europe was extremely interested in the events transpiring in the Americas during the first century of the Spanish and Portuguese conquest of the New World. Also of great interest was the fact that the world's mightiest army was encountering such savage resistance from warriors who faced them with crude weapons.

La Araucana is an epic poem that lacks the single hero associated with the genre. On the other hand, two abstract heroes stand out: the Spaniard and the Araucanian. This dual hero was to be profoundly imprinted in the national psyche, forging a lasting image of Chileans as composed of the best of two distinct cultures which, together, would mold a new nation. Ercilla's positive presentation of both Spaniard and Indian would go far in establishing the duality of the Chilean character, a blend of the European and the native American, without the cultural and historical rancor that has existed in some of the nations of Latin America, notably in Mexico. The verses from *La Araucana*, quoted in translation at the beginning of this book, demonstrate the poet's admiration of both the nation of Chile and its native inhabitants. Its laudatory tone has left a deep imprint on the national consciousness.

ANDRÉS BELLO

Diego de Portales, businessman and politician, set the course for the relative political stability which has made Chile a model among the nations of Latin America. But there is another individual who, almost single-handedly, founded or helped to found many of the institutions that have molded the nation into what it is today. This role fell to Andrés Bello, a Venezuelan who made Chile his residence during the last thirty-seven years of his long life.

Bello, a good friend of Simón Bolívar, was born in Caracas in 1781, while the country was still a Spanish colony. Often likened to Benjamin Franklin, Bello also lived in England for nineteen years, studying there and preparing himself for the practice of law. Even though he was invited to return to Venezuela by Bolívar, he chose not to do so and instead, moved to Chile, at the age of forty-eight, at the invitation of the government. There he served in the Ministry of Foreign Affairs and edited the official newspaper, *El Monitor Araucano* (The Araucanian Monitor). He remained there until his death in 1865, at the age of almost eighty-four.

He founded the Colegio de Santiago (Santiago School) and was the first president of the Universidad de Chile, which opened its doors in 1842. His principal works were the nation's Código Civil (Civil Code) and *Gramática de la lengua castellana* (Grammar of the Spanish Language), probably the most significant such grammar since the first one, written by Antonio de Nebrija, in 1492.

In the literary field, Bello was both poet and essayist. His *La agricultura de la Zona Tórrida* (Agriculture of the Torrid Zone) attempts to Americanize and poeticize the New World, thus turning the eyes of contemporary artists toward the originality of their American environment. Many of his contemporary critics were on an almost rabid course directed at separating the new nations of America from Spain, both culturally and politically. Bello, even as he attempted to point out the originality of the New World, did not wish to break the bonds which had given him and Spanish America the language, religion, and laws of Spain. His essay "El Castellano en América" (Spanish in America), taken from his *Gramática de la lengua castellana*, which he completed in 1847, pointed out that the New World should not exhibit a servile attitude toward Spain, but should instead feel free to reflect its own originality while maintaining the strength and value of the language. In the essay he writes: "I do not pretend to write for the Castilians. My lessons are directed at my brothers, the inhabitants of Spanish America. I feel it is important to conserve the language of our forefathers in as pure a manner as possible, as a providential means of communication and as a bond of fraternity among the many nations of Spanish origin that are scattered on two continents" (Gómez-Gil, 235).

Those who sought to break with the uniformity of the Spanish of Spain, among them the Chilean writer Victorino Lastarria, waged a long but ultimately fruitless battle for the creation of an independent Chilean Spanish. The linguistic battle did not officially end in Chile until 1910. Spanish today is uniform throughout Latin America and Spain. Still, the New World has contributed much to the growth of Spanish, both in America and in Spain, for of the 400 million speakers of the language, more than 90 percent are in Latin America and the United States.

By the middle of the nineteenth century, Chile had became a center of culture. Exiles from other parts of Latin America, especially Argentine writer and thinker Domingo Faustino Sarmiento, settled for long periods of time in Chile and created a highly stimulating environment for the exchange of ideas. Bello and Sarmiento, both intellectuals of the highest caliber, differed greatly in their political, cultural, and pedagogical ideals. In 1842, a controversy arose between them that clearly expressed their differences and perspectives on Spanish American intellectualism. Sarmiento, a self-taught liberal and a proponent of public education, defended a progressive concept of culture and the romantic freedom of expression; he was also an ardent lover of the models presented by France and its intellectual ideals. Bello, on the other hand, advocated an aristocratic concept of literary values, favored the linguistic purity of the Spanish language, and admired the value of Spanish culture.

El Mercurio of Valparaíso and *El Semanario Literario* (The Literary Weekly), another newspaper, became forums for the attacks that Sarmiento and his advocates, and Bello and his, loosed upon one other. Bello, the product of a solid, classical education, living in a politically stable nation, faced Sarmiento, a romantic intellectual, an exile from the tyranny of Argentine dictator Juan Manuel de Rosas. They differed greatly in their perceptions of the nature of literature and culture, but their often acerbic polemic served to turn the middle of the century into a highly stimulating period from which, in the long run, Chile and its intellectual inheritance profited profoundly.

Sarmiento, an admirer of Horace Mann, the American educator and proponent of public education, went back to Argentina after the fall of Rosas in 1852. There he was instrumental in the establishment of a system of public education and wrote his famous *Civilización y barbarie* (Civilization and Barbarism). In 1868 he was elected president of Argentina.

ALBERTO BLEST GANA

One of the greatest novelists in the realism movement in Spanish America was a Chilean, Alberto Blest Gana (1830–1920). His greatest ambition was to be known as the Balzac of Chile. (Honoré de Balzac [1799–1850] was a French novelist whose works provided a comprehensive view of French life.)

Balzac's more than ninety novels, to which he gave the umbrella title of *La Comédie humaine* (The Human Comedy), were an inspiration to Blest Gana, who attempted to depict what he perceived to be the reality of the human condition in his own country. Blest Gana was intimately acquainted with French literature, since he lived in France for some fifty of his ninety years of life.

Blest Gana's novels provide a detailed document of Chilean society, from the period of the reconquista (the Reconquest), when Spain returned to reconquer Chile after the defeat of Napoleon in Europe, to the author's present. He was a careful observer of national life and a good depicter of social customs. Those who wish to understand the formation of the aristocracy, the middle class, and the poor class in Chile would do well to turn to the novels of Blest Gana.

Durante la reconquista (During the Reconquest), published in 1897, describes the city of Santiago between 1814 and 1818, when victorious Spanish troops defeated Carrera and O'Higgins. Ridiculous and sinister Spanish generals are depicted even as heroic patriots and picturesque *rotos* (roguish and picaresque members of the lower class) ambulate through the pages of the novel.

Los transplantados (The Transplanted), which appeared in 1904, concerns decadent members of the upper class who live a life of debauchery in Paris, having abandoned Chile to better themselves by marrying into European nobility. The only outcome of their search is that they come to be referred to as *rastaquouères* (a derogatory term that means "flashy adventurers").

Undoubtedly the best work by Blest Gana is the novel *Martín Rivas* (1862), an admirable literary fresco that portrays the marriage of a middle-class man, Martín, who marries into Santiago's aristocracy during the middle of the nineteenth century. The period's society is described in minute detail: the importance of money and politics; the struggle between *pipiolos* (greenhorns or novices) and *pelucones* (literally, bigwigs), the terms used to refer to Liberals and Conservatives, respectively; the divisions among the classes: *rotos* (lower and inferior class), *gente de medio pelo* (middle class, literally "people with middle-length hair," thus, not bigwigs), and *gente decente* (moneyed people, literally "decent people"); the influence of French society and customs among the wealthy, and their opportunism and moral dissoluteness. The reader is also treated to descriptions of private parties, popular festivals, political meetings, religious ceremonies, and public markets. The novel attempts to provide a faithful slice of life in the capital of Chile, just as Balzac had done for France.

BALDOMERO LILLO

Baldomero Lillo (1867–1923) is acknowledged as the first Chilean writer to demonstrate a serious concern with the social problems that existed in Chile between the 1890s and the early 1900s. He had delved deeply into the writings of the naturalist Russian and French writers, and the influence of Fyodor Dostoyevsky and, especially, of Emile Zola's *Germinal* is evident in his short stories.

Lillo was born in the mining town of Lota, in the province of Concepción, and belonged to Chile's middle class. His work consists of a sonnet written as a very young man, some forty-two short stories, one article, and two chapters of a novel that he never completed. Two collections of short stories, to which he gave the Latin titles *Sub terra* (Under the Earth) and *Sub sole* (Under the Sun), appeared in 1904 and 1907, respectively. The first one contains short narratives that are philosophical parables describing contemporary customs, and is the collection for which Lillo achieved national and continental acclaim.

The stories in *Sub terra* are based on Lillo's direct observation of the life of the coal miners of southern Chile, among whom he worked for a while. Some of the best of these stories are "El chiflón del diablo" (The Devil's Draft), "La compuerta número 12" (Gate Number 12), and "El grisú" (Firedamp [a combustible gas consisting chiefly of methane; it forms especially in coal mines]). With sharp realism and vigorous protest, Lillo depicts the horrible working conditions of Chilean coal miners at the turn of the century. His stories helped to awaken the interest of other writers and to make the authorities aware of those conditions. Many consider him the father of Chilean realism.

It has long been said that Chile is a land of poets. This view has been supported by some and rejected by others, the latter perhaps fearful that prose narrative might appear to be slighted by such an assertion. Still, it is significant that the country's first major work was in verse (*La Araucana*) and that its two winners of the Nobel Prize for literature have been in that genre, the first being the first Spanish American to receive that coveted award. Vicente Huidobro, Gabriela Mistral, and Pablo Neruda are the three most significant twentieth-century poets from Chile.

VICENTE HUIDOBRO

The well-deserved fame of Mistral and Neruda has somewhat dimmed the literary importance of Vicente Huidobro (1893–1948), but modern criticism has rediscovered him, recognizing his importance within the *vanguardista* (the avant-garde, modernist) movement. The movement itself, *vanguardismo*, reached its fullness in the early 1920s. Like most new literary movements, it sought to break new ground by leaving aside the past. It focused on the originality of the present, worshiping the metaphor, creating audacious images, and seeking to give expression to what had never been expressed. The poetry created sometimes seems to be devoid of any sense, especially if analyzed by means of the usual and commonplace. It bears some resemblance, at least in its desire to attract through synesthesia (generally, the confluence of all the senses), to the poetry of the earlier *modernistas* of Spanish America (1888–early twentieth century). Some poems, for example, attempted to imitate the sounds produced by insects or by falling water; others were written in the shape of the poem's images. In "Canto IV," Huidobro plays with words, creating what might at first appear to be nonsensical derivations of an authentic word in Spanish, but at the same time intimating diverse meanings that do or might make sense.

Beginning with the beautiful image of the swallow (*golondrina*, in Spanish), he changes *golondrina* to *golonfina, goloncima, golonchina, golonniña,* and other variations, each connoting something different. The suffixes all have meanings of their own or intimate certain images that add to the original *golondrina*. For example, *fina* means fine; *cima* means mountaintop; *china* means China or Chinese; *clima* means climate; *niña* means girl; and so on. The poem thus attracts the reader/listener linguistically as well as audibly.

Huidobro was able to devote himself to poetry, without the usual economic concerns of many artists, because he was a man of means. He lived for long periods in Spain and France and was even a candidate for the presidency of Chile in 1925. The aim of his new aesthetic theory, known as *creacionismo* (creationism), was to create poetry which had no links whatsoever to the known, external world. His verse formed a new reality, one which could not be explained by or seen within the context of what the world knows and accepts as real. Huidobro said that when he wrote, his trees, his mountains, his rivers, and his oceans would be solely his, not nature's. He would not be subservient to it, but independent of it. His *Altazor o viaje en paracaídas* (Altazor or a Voyage in a Parachute) was written in 1931. In it he reveals his metaphysical anguish, his sadness, and his skepticism. He shows what to him is the irrationality of life by, among other things, the irrationality

A beautiful mosaic honoring South America's first Nobel Prize laureate in literature, Chile's Gabriela Mistral. It is above the sidewalk on Santiago's main thoroughfare, the busy Alameda.

of his verse forms, which lack rhyme and uniformity of length. Huidobro followed no schools; he created his own. Standing apart from many who have acknowledged the inspiration of others before them, he set his own course; others imitated him and, by doing so, acknowledged his well-deserved place in Chilean poetry.

GABRIELA MISTRAL

Gabriela Mistral, the literary pen name of Lucila Godoy Alcayaga, was born in 1889. She is recognized, today, more than forty years after her death, as one of the most lyrical poets writing in the Spanish language. Born in Elqui, in the province of Coquimbo, north of Santiago, Mistral was a teacher in elementary and secondary schools. In 1922, the minister of education of Mexico, José Vasconcelos, invited her to that country to act as a consultant in the educational reform that he championed. In 1925, she entered the Chilean diplomatic corps and served as consul or cultural attaché in various countries of Europe and in the United States. She died in Roslyn, New York, in 1957.

Mistral wrote poems and narratives for children, lyrical verse, and prose.

Some of her serenades, children's stories, and lullabies are among the most beautiful in the Spanish language. Still, it is as a poet that Mistral is especially recognized. Her main theme is love: love for mankind, for the universe, God, nature, justice, the poor, the forgotten, and children. When she was seventeen, she fell in love with a man who committed suicide, apparently on a point of honor. This tragic love was to mark the course of her poetry. She never married, and thus was never able to achieve her double dream of erotic and maternal love. Her best book, *Desolación* (Desolation), which appeared in 1922, expounds her deep sadness and solitude, born out of the loss of her beloved. It is the bittersweet expression of love lost, never to be regained. In 1924, she completed *Ternura* (Tenderness), the love expressed here being *agape* (from the Greek), love toward fellow humans, children, the poor, the persecuted, and the forgotten. Mistral's verse is always profound, tender, and sincere. The love she expresses in her poetry is more spiritual than sensual. In 1945, Mistral became the first Chilean, the first Spanish American, and the first woman writing in Spanish to receive the Nobel Prize for literature. A beautiful poem titled "Meciendo" (Rocking) provides a beautiful example of her love for children and her appreciation of God and nature. The verb "to rock," employed in reference to a child, is blended with the wind's rocking of the sea or its blowing over fields of wheat.

PABLO NERUDA

In 1971, twenty-six years after Mistral received Latin America's first Nobel Prize for literature, another Chilean poet, Pablo Neruda (1904–1973), was equally honored. His real name had been Ricardo Neftalí Reyes Basoalto; he took the pseudonym of Neruda in 1920, at the age of sixteen. He had met Mistral in the southern Chilean city of Temuco and admired her work greatly.

Neruda is considered one of the most significant poets of the twentieth century. Already well known in Chile when he received the Nobel Prize, two years before his death, the poet and his work achieved international renown as a result of the award. The mid-1990s Italian movie *Il Postino* (The Postman) has brought him and his work renewed fame and attention. Based on a fictitious sojourn by the poet in Italy, the film is replete with the significance of his poetry and the process of its creation.

Critics have divided his work into five cycles, each depicting a different period of his literary work. *Crepusculario* (Twilight, 1923) belongs to the first cycle. It combines simplicity with the feelings of the poet, as does *Veinte poemas de amor y una canción desesperada* (Twenty Poems of Love and a Song of Despair, 1924). The latter is Neruda's most popular work. In the composition of these poems, he was inspired by two women, one from Santiago and the other from Temuco, both unidentified. His love poems are marked by feelings of abandonment and solitude, both recurrent themes throughout his work. Other well-known collections are *Residencia en la tierra* (Residence on Earth), Part I (1933) and Part II (1935), both of which belong to the second cycle. They reflect the years he spent abroad, holding several diplomatic posts in Asia. It was his surrealistic period, during which he observed the problems of the world. He expresses his existential angst, his indignation in the face of injustice. His poem "Walking Around" (title originally in English) is a good example of this period.

Some of Neruda's most down-to-earth poems are in his *Odas elementales* (Elementary Odes); 1954. The poet turns to the everyday, the commonplace, in order to describe it in great and precise detail. Each selection bears a title such as "Oda a la alcachofa" (Ode to the Artichoke) or "Oda a los calcetines" (Ode to Socks). Lowly, everyday items are described with affection, with the appreciation of someone who accepts their merit and worth. Neruda left fascinating memoirs titled *Confieso que he vivido* (I Confess That I Have Lived), which appeared posthumously in 1974.

Poem 20 of *Veinte poemas de amor* is one of the best remembered. The following lines provide a good example of his lyricism:

> I can write the saddest verses this night.
> I can write, for example: The night is laden with stars, and the
> blue heavenly bodies tremble, faraway.
> I can write the saddest verses this night.
> I loved her, and at times she loved me as well.
> (translation by G. I. Castillo-Feliú)

"Walking Around" is an existential poem with which the reader can easily identify. The following lines are scattered through the entire poem:

> It so happens that I get tired of being a man.
> The smell of barbershops makes me bawl out loud.
> It so happens that I get tired of my feet and my nails and my
> hair and my shadow.
> It so happens that I get tired of being a man.
> (translation by G. I. Castillo-Feliú)

"Oda a los calcetines" succeeds in ennobling a simple pair of socks; they are no longer articles of clothing that the wearer mechanically puts on. The poem loosely takes the shape of the socks themselves. The following is an English translation:

> Maru Mori brought me
>   a pair
>   of socks
> which she knit with her shepherd's
>   hands,
>   two socks as soft
>   as hares.
>   Inside them
>   I put my feet
>   as if inside
>   two
>   etuis
>   knitted with threads from the
>   twilight of the day . . .
>   (translation by G. I. Castillo-Feliú)

Neruda loved Isla Negra (Black Island) on the coast of Chile not far from Valparaíso; there the poet spent many a day, writing some of the beautiful poems that feature prominently in his work. He spent most of the last days of his life there; terminally ill, he was moved to Santiago only shortly before he died in late September 1973, some two weeks after the coup that toppled the government of Salvador Allende, whose friend and short-lived political opponent he had been (Allende belonged to the Socialist party; Neruda had long been a member of the Communist party of Chile).

PEDRO PRADO

Perhaps the best writer of the artistic novel in Chile is Pedro Prado (1886–1952), also a distinguished poet, a fact that is easily discernible in his prose works. A great admirer of Leo Tolstoy, Prado founded and presided over the famous "Group of Ten," an association of painters, poets, musicians, and architects who, under the inspiration of the Russian master, met for several years at Prado's house in the outskirts of Santiago to share their common aesthetic interests.

In *Un juez rural* (A Country Judge), published in 1924, Prado analyzes the dilemma encountered by a country judge who attempts to administer justice by following the dictates of his own conscience, even if they run contrary to the rigid penal code that he has sworn to uphold. An interesting predicament that he encounters is very vexing to him: it is impossible to be individually just, for when one punishes the one who is guilty of a crime, one also punishes his mother, his wife, and his children. Thus, the judge feels that in order to be just, he must reward what is good even as he punishes what is bad. It proves to be a catch-22 situation that he is unable to surmount.

The novel *Alsino* (1920) is undoubtedly Prado's masterpiece. It can be interpreted at many levels and can be appreciated by readers of various ages: some critics have classified it as a fairy tale, some as an allegory, and still others as a work of transcendental symbolism. It is the tale of a young lad, Alsino, who dreams of flying, falls from a tree during an attempt to do so, and is left hunchbacked as a result. With time, his malformed back develops into wings and Alsino is, indeed, able to fly. From that moment on, the lad soars and returns to earth, providing the reader with the amazing perspectives that flying affords him and with many adventures that are at times comical, at times sad, and at times edifying. The last few pages of the novel show a clear parallel between Alsino and Icarus, as the author's prose soars as high as Alsino's wings can propel him:

> It was the month of May, a month of fleeting stars. Mingled with those that fell that night, no one would have been able to discern him.
>
> One league before touching the earth, of Alsino there was only impalpable ash. Lacking the weight needed to continue falling, it floated aimlessly, like a shred of fog, until daybreak. The dawn breezes took care of dispersing them. (translation by G. I. Castillo-Feliú)

Prado employs Alsino's magical power to interpret the reality of Chile's south with exquisite lyricism. Using his talents as prose writer and poet, Prado succeeds in creating a beautiful work of art that stands as one of Chile's most enduring works of literature.

EDUARDO BARRIOS

Eduardo Barrios (1884–1963) was born of a Chilean father and a Peruvian mother, and lived in several of the countries of Spanish America. He worked as a salesman, explorer, circus performer, and weightlifter. He finally settled in Chile, where he served as director of the National Library and minister of education. His literary work does not reflect any particular school, for he exhibited a truly individualistic style, writing, as he himself stated, as "a man of feeling."

Many of his best works, whether novel or short story, display a deep understanding of what, for lack of a better term, could be described as sentimental abnormality. His three novels are penetrating studies of the "sentimental abnormalities" of children and of a monk. Barrios's protagonists are beings whose emotional nature is so fragile that they are unable to cope with the stresses of life, and fall into madness or spiritual disintegration.

In *Un perdido* (A Lost One), which appeared in 1918, Barrios deals with an abnormally sensitive child who lives a life of failure and discordance in an urban setting. He follows the model of the nineteenth-century French writer Gustave Flaubert, with his child protagonist Frédéric Moreau in *L'Éducation sentimentale* (The Sentimental Education).

El hermano asno (translated as *Brother Ass*), which Barrios published in 1922, takes its title from the term used by St. Francis of Assisi to designate the body. Said to be based on true events, the novel narrates the story of Brother Lázaro, a saintly friar who struggles against the sin of pride and uses a sin of the flesh to humble himself before all those who praise his humility and saintliness. Barrios obtained permission from the abbot at the St. Francis Church and monastery in Santiago to spend time in a friar's cell, so that he could provide an accurate description of his protagonist's surroundings.

The novella *El niño que enloqueció de amor* (The Child Who Went Mad from Love), which Barrios published in 1915, purports to be the diary of a ten-year-old boy who falls madly in love with Angélica, his mother's best friend. The impossibility of such a relationship causes Angélica to reject the child's attraction to her and the boy's ultimate fall into a state of insanity. Barrios thus creates an interesting study of psychological abnormality, using the novel as his vehicle. In the novel, he employs a beautiful metaphor to describe the case, comparing the child's amorous attraction to that of a young bird who is prematurely awakened by a moonbeam as it slumbers on a tree branch in the middle of the night.

JOAQUÍN EDWARDS BELLO

Joaquín Edwards Bello (1887–1968) might have been Chile's greatest novelist, according to a critic, if he had not insisted on stressing the most sordid aspects of life in the city. In this he was certainly showing the influence of his French master, the naturalist Émile Zola. He tended to observe all of his protagonists in accordance with preconceived concepts of how they should be: they fit the mold that he had conceived before he set out to write. Nevertheless, Edwards Bello is the principal exponent of the novel of the city, and his creations, though tending to be caricatures, provide the best descriptions of ghetto life, especially in the capital.

The best of his works is the novel *El roto* (1920), an excellent character study about a social type that is quintessentially Chilean. Although the topic is necessarily limited, for the *roto's* two basic necessities are food and alcohol, the novel has special value as a social document that attempts to explain the reality of this outcast of Chilean society.

MARIANO LATORRE

Mariano Latorre (1886–1955) is the best representative of the Chilean regionalist school. Those who read his short stories and novels come away with a clear picture of the natural and human reality of Chile. In his first collections of short stories, *Paisajes chilenos* (Chilean Landscapes), which was published in 1910, and *Cuentos del Maule* (Stories from the Maule), published two years later, Latorre provides a detailed description of Chile's geography; character description, dialogue, and plot are subordinated to the scenery. Later, his writing matured and he gradually overcame these deficiencies. *Cuna de cóndores* (Condors' Nest), published in 1918, shows the influence of France's master of the short story, Guy de Maupassant, and of the latter's compatriot, the Decadent Joris Karl Huysmans. Among Latorre's later works are *Chilenos del mar* (Chileans of the Sea), which appeared in 1929 and focused on those who make their living along the coast, and *Chile, país de rincones* (Chile, Country of Corners), which was published the year of his death. In his later works, Latorre never abandons his great interest in and admiration for Chile's natural beauty and reality, but he focuses much more on character and plot development than he had done in the early years of his literary life. Still, he maintains his interest in blending nature and humanity: for him, *huasos* (country people) and hunters are inextricably linked with the natural environment in which their lives unfold.

MANUEL ROJAS

Manuel Rojas (1896–1973) was born in Argentina of Chilean parents, and after working on the Transandean railroad for a few years, he moved to Chile at the age of twenty-four and settled there. Like others of his literary compatriots, Rojas was a jack-of-all-trades, working at jobs that included theater prompter, watchman, stevedore, sailor, actor, and wall painter. He later became a journalist, an official at the National Library, and a university professor. Many of his work experiences provided him with the material for some of his best works of fiction.

In 1957, Rojas received the National Prize for Literature. In the early 1960s, he was a visiting professor at several U.S. universities. His works represent a break with regionalism for its own sake, attempting to move Chilean narrative beyond regionalism by using modern literary techniques without putting aside the life experiences that had made him what he was.

His first verses appeared in the literary magazine *Los Diez*, which had been created by Pedro Prado and his circle of friends. In 1926, Rojas published a collection of short stories, *Hombres del sur* (Men from the South), which contained several stories that had already received wide recognition and literary awards. In 1929, a second collection of stories, *El delincuente* (The Delinquent), was published. It contained one of the most anthologized short stories in the Spanish language, "El vaso de leche" (The Glass of Milk). For this heart-warming story, Rojas certainly drew on his own experiences as sailor and stevedore, creating the story of a young stowaway who is cast off a ship in a Chilean port, without any means of sustenance. Those around him, however, in spite of being hardened by the environment, provide support for this lost young man and imbue him with hope for the future.

In 1951, Rojas published one of the masterpieces of Spanish American literature, the novel *Hijo de ladrón* (Son of a Thief). The work appears to use the technique of the Spanish picaresque novel of the late sixteenth and early seventeenth centuries, with its first-person narrator, its many episodes, and its adventures. But it abounds in the use of interior monologue, the juxtaposition of narratives, counterpoint, breaks in chronology, flashbacks—techniques that had become standard in the fiction of the first half of the twentieth century. The novel is a study of a protagonist experiencing conflict between his individual degradation and society's expectations.

María Luisa Bombal

María Luisa Bombal (1910–1980) was a novelist and short story writer who achieved great renown for works that delved deeply into the feminine soul. Her two novels, *La última niebla* (translated by Bombal as *House of Mist* in 1947), published in 1935, and *La amortajada* (translated by Bombal as *The Shrouded Woman* in 1948), published in 1938, preceded the establishment of surrealism by at least ten years, and have placed her among Chile's best-known writers.

One of Bombal's short stories, "El árbol" (The Tree), published in 1939, has been anthologized in countless books, both in Spanish and in translation.

One of the best ways to enjoy the story is to accompany its reading with the music of Mozart, Beethoven, and Chopin. Bombal uses their compositions to mirror the young protagonist's existence at three different stages of her life: the childhood years (Mozart's playful, crystalline notes); the romance, passion, and effervescence of youth (Beethoven); and the nostalgic, melancholy years of her disillusionment (Chopin). It is one of the most finely wrought short narratives artistically using the technique of point and counterpoint to move back and forth between the depiction of life and music.

THE "BOOM" IN LATIN AMERICAN LITERATURE

A little more than a decade after the end of World War II, there was a period during which Latin American literature experienced tremendous growth. This great spurt in literature was given the onomatopoeic name "boom," for novels of significant quality were rapidly being penned by writers throughout Latin America. Their books could be found throughout the world, and literary circles were beginning to turn their eyes to an area with which they were not familiar.

Aside from the already-mentioned Pablo Neruda and Gabriela Mistral, three other writers from North, Central, and South America were honored with the Nobel Prize for literature and several others have been perennial nominees. Gabriel García Márquez, of Colombia, is undoubtedly the best known of them and his seminal work, *Cien años de soledad* (One Hundred Years of Solitude), which appeared in Spanish in 1967, is known the world over, both in its Spanish original and in its excellent translation. This sudden surge in writing from the part of Latin American writers has produced a veritable school of translators who, on the whole, have become very adept at their trade and who have opened the world of Latin American writers to many who would, otherwise, be unable to appreciate such rich literature in the original.

ISABEL ALLENDE

It is said by many critics that contemporary literature in Spanish America can be divided between works that preceded Gabriel García Márquez's *One Hundred Years of Solitude* and works that followed it. When Chilean writer Isabel Allende (b. 1942) published her first work, *La casa de los espíritus* (The House of the Spirits), in 1982, some critics saw the book as nothing more than a paraphrasing of García Márquez's novel. There are, indeed, many similarities in style and imagery that easily remind the reader of the Colombian's earlier book. But Allende's first work, and her many subsequent works, have tremendous merit of their own, and their popularity has made her as well known as her Colombian counterpart.

Isabel Allende is the niece of Salvador Allende (president of Chile 1970–1973), and there is no doubt that this factor helped her to be recognized in the field of contemporary fiction. It is her own merit, however, that has placed her prominently among the great figures of contemporary Latin American literature.

La casa de los espíritus is a family saga for which the author drew upon her own history, as she has freely admitted. It is possible, for those acquainted with Allende's family tree, to draw parallels between many of the characters of this first novel and members of her family. What is depicted, in essence, is the saga of a patriarchal and authoritarian family from the nineteenth century through the twentieth. The climactic moments of the novel focus on the years leading up to the Popular Unity government of Salvador Allende, the coup d'état that toppled him in 1973, and the effects of the early years of the military dictatorship that ensued. A film version of *The House of the Spirits*, made in 1993, helped to make Allende's work better known to the public.

Several other works have emerged from Allende's pen. *De amor y de sombra* (Of Love and Shadows) appeared in 1984. It focused on the Pinochet dictatorship and on a true case of political violence, the murder of five members of one family. After this second work, Allende abandoned themes associated with the years of dictatorship.

Eva Luna (1987) and *Los cuentos de Eva Luna* (The Stories of Eva Luna), which appeared in 1990, present strong, free, and adventurous feminine characters. In all these early works, the language is rich and the characters are representative of the contemporary creations of Latin American writers who freely blend reality and magical realism.

Allende had left Chile in 1975, shortly after the coup d'état that toppled Salvador Allende, and settled in Caracas, Venezuela, where she prepared the manuscript of *La casa de los espíritus*. She moved to the United States shortly thereafter, and in 1991 she published *El plan infinito* (The Infinite Plan), whose action takes place in California during the Vietnam War and after. It marks a departure from her earlier works because the setting and characters are no longer associated with Latin America and the concerns that had marked her work from 1982 through 1990.

A personal tragedy provides the background for *Paula* (1994), which depicts the author's relationship with her daughter and the mysterious illness that ultimately took the latter's life. With *Afrodita* (Aphrodite), published in 1998, Allende joins other writers, such as Mexico's Laura Esquivel (*Like*

Water for Chocolate, 1989; English translation in 1992), in combining the sensual pleasures of eating with literature, history, and love. Her latest work, *Hija de la Fortuna* (Daughter of Fortune) is set in Chile and California at the time of the gold rush.

José Donoso

José Donoso (1924–1996), often included among the writers of the "boom," hobnobbed with many of the writers in that group. Born to a well-to-do family in Santiago, Donoso was considered to be the black sheep of the family, turning away from the path that someone of his social standing was expected to follow. He attended one of Santiago's most select schools but dropped out before completing his studies due to inattentiveness and lack of direction. He left the capital and traveled south to work as a shepherd. In spite of his early lack of interest in things academic, Donoso did learn English well and obtained a scholarship that allowed him to travel to the United States and attend Princeton University, where he earned a B.A. in English. While at Princeton, he wrote two short stories in English that were published in *Manuscripts*, the university literary magazine.

Upon his return to Chile, Donoso began an illustrious literary career which included the writing of several short stories and novels between 1954 and 1997, his last work being published posthumously. His first novel, *Coronación* (Coronation), appeared in 1957, and describes the indecisive life of a man in his fifties, who lives with an aristocratic grandmother and countless servants. A second novel, titled *Este domingo* (This Sunday), published in 1966, is composed of two parts, each narrated from a different point of view. Donoso was often considered for the Nobel Prize.

Without a doubt, Donoso's *El obsceno pájaro de la noche* (The Obscene Bird of Night), published in 1970 in Barcelona, where the author was living, established him as one of that select group of writers which included García Márquez, the Mexican Carlos Fuentes, and the Peruvian Mario Vargas Llosa. The novel, which takes its title from a work by one of Donoso's favorite authors, Henry James, appeared late in 1970 and placed him irrevocably upon the list of universally recognized Latin American writers. Like many of his literary contemporaries, Donoso chose exile from his native land, not for political reasons but out of a desire to move away from his personal and familial demons. Writing about Chile from the perspective afforded by his residence in Spain, Donoso was able to exorcise those emotions which had motivated his writing since the first short stories in English. In 1980, he returned to Chile, residing and writing there until his death sixteen years later.

6

The Performing Arts

CHILE'S RICH, ETHNIC CRUCIBLE has contributed greatly to the performing arts. The nation's European and native roots are clearly evident in its music, both classical and folkloric, in its dance, and in the theater. In the field of music, composers and performers alike evidence an appreciation for Beethoven, Mozart, and Bach and, increasingly, for the haunting lyricism of the music of the Andes, popular around the world since the 1960s. Folksingers employ the old-world guitar to create music that brings social inequities, borne out of the clash of the European and the native, to the national consciousness. The theater, as well, instructs even as it entertains the public, reflecting the reality of the times. In short, Chile's diverse cultures are increasingly well represented in the artistic manifestations of its artists in a manner that demonstrates the nation's awakened awareness of its multifaceted past.

THE *CUECA*

The *cueca*, Chile's national dance, is associated with people in the countryside, and since the early years of the republic has been linked with the independence celebrations on September 18. It is danced all across the nation, with many choreographic variations. It can be a reenactment of the cock's courting of the hen, the amorous wooing of a couple, or even the attempt of a *huaso* (Chilean cowboy) to lasso a young mare. The man and the woman dance around one another, brandishing handkerchiefs, in step to music played by instruments such as the guitar, the harp, and the accordion, as one or more singers tell a story.

In a formal version of the *cueca*, the *huaso* is dressed in black pants and a shirt. He also wears a short poncho that comes halfway down his chest; a wide *faja* (sash) with fringed ends that is usually red, white, and blue, reflecting Chile's flag; and a black felt hat that resembles the Cordoban hat worn in Andalusia, the brim no wider than a cowboy's hat but the crown significantly narrower. On his feet he wears black boots to which large spurs are attached. There is something of the flamenco in the man's repeated *zapateo* (tapping with the boots) on a floor that resounds doubly, for the sound emanates as much from the boots' heels as from the jingling spurs. As the couple dances and the singers sing, the spectators may be moved to emit a high-pitched sound that resembles the Spanish trilled *r*.

FOLK MUSIC

Chile's history is a significant component of its culture, and its music reflects this quite clearly. Various songs or tunes commemorate historical events or popular celebrations rooted in history. Among them are the *tonada* (ballad), the *canción* (tune, song), the *cueca*, and the *vals* (waltz). The *tonada* is the form most employed for ballads with a cultural or historical background. A well-known *tonada* has the *cueca* as its topic and title.

In the early 1960s, an album was recorded by a musical group called Silvia Infanta y los Baqueanos (loosely translated as Silvia Infanta and the Rangers), with the title, *Música para la historia de Chile* (Music Featuring Chile's History). The album contained twelve tunes, four of which were ballads reflecting Chile's struggle for independence. One was titled "La Independencia de Chile" (Chile's Independence); the rest were songs praising three of Chile's heroes of independence: Manuel Rodríguez, Bernardo O'Higgins, and the Carrera brothers, José Miguel and Luis.

The appearance and popularity of these ballads reflected the fact that 150 years after independence, the public was hungry for a deeper understanding of the conflict between O'Higgins and the Carreras during the second decade of the nineteenth century, and of the divisions that had existed between these two factions struggling for Chile's independence from Spain. The ballads celebrating the Carreras bring to the fore the struggle between them and O'Higgins, and the true nature of José Miguel's death (shot treacherously in the back, as the song states).

Perhaps the most beloved group of folk singers in Chile is the foursome Huasos Quincheros, popular for more than thirty years; their repertoire focuses on Chile's people, natural beauty, and folklore. Some of their *canciones* or *tonadas* reflect types that are fast disappearing, such as "El frutero" (The Fruit Seller). Others celebrate the beauty of the nation, "Chile lindo" (Beautiful Chile) or the singularity of the national dance, "¡Dónde habrá como mi cueca!" (Where Could There Be a Dance as Grand as the Cueca!). There is also the hauntingly nostalgic "Río, Río" (River, River), which features a forlorn lover who imagines that the flowing river he contemplates is laden with the tears he is shedding for his lost love.

Some of the Huasos Quincheros' ballads and songs describe the beautiful and colorful costumes typically worn by people in the country, as in "Manta de tres colores" (Three-Colored Poncho), or the guitar, which is always the lead instrument in Chilean music, as in "El cantar de mi guitarra" (loosely translated as "The Music of My Guitar"). The *tonada* recognized internationally as typically Chilean is "Yo vendo unos negros" (loosely translated as "Black Eyes for Sale"), in which the singer is despondent over the black-eyed beauty who has forsaken him for another.

Andean Music

Years ago, when the song "El cóndor pasa" (The Condor Flies) was a popular hit, the world became aware of the haunting and original music of the Andean countries, especially Peru, Ecuador, and Bolivia. Inti Illimani, one of the best-known bands that specialize in music of this region, however, is Chilean. It was formed in 1967 in Chile and moved to Europe some six years later. Guamary, another band that originated in Chile, has since disbanded.

These two bands, like all Andean groups, use instruments that are indigenous to South America. The panpipes, known as *zampoñas*, are made from bamboo and come in several sizes, ranging from perhaps two to three inches to some that are almost as tall as the musician. The sounds produced can be extremely high or low, depending on the length of each pipe. Some *zampoñas* have all the notes necessary for a particular melody, so that one musician can play it alone. The most common arrangement, though, is to have two or three *zampoñas* played by three musicians, alternating in the production of the notes. There is great beauty and artistry in the coordination displayed by the musicians as each plays one note, immediately followed by other notes produced by other musicians.

A second pre-Columbian instrument is the *quena*, a cane flute that can vary in size. The *ocarina*, another wind instrument, is made of clay and has the shape of a turtle's back. It can vary in size, providing a great range of sounds as well. The *palo de lluvia* (rain stick) produces a constant sound that resembles the sound of falling rain; it, too, varies in length and sound.

The Andean music of today is not exactly the same as that which existed in pre-Columbian times, since most modern groups also use instruments that represent the contributions of later civilizations. Among the instruments introduced by Spain is, of course, the guitar and its many derivatives. The *tiple* is an instrument of Colombian origin, with four strings that produce a sound not unlike a harpsichord. Common in the Andes and elsewhere in South America is the *charango*, a mandolin-like instrument which has an armadillo shell as the sounding board.

Typical percussion instruments are the tambourine, of various origins, and drums such as the *bombo*, originally of African origin and made from a hollowed-out tree trunk. Although those who hear Andean music usually think of Peru, Ecuador, and Bolivia, there is a commonality between the indigenous peoples of those three nations and those of Chile, a fact which Chile has acknowledged and celebrated since the 1960s. The Mapuches (Araucanians) were the indigenous people that Valdivia and others encountered in the Central Valley in 1541, but the Incas had come into contact with them before the arrival of the Spanish, and had clashed with them as well. This renewed interest in Andean music has helped produce a rapprochement among the Andean nations.

Violeta Parra

Violeta Parra (1917–1967) was the sister of the renowned poet Nicanor Parra, author of *Antipoemas* (Anti Poems). Associated with liberal causes, Violeta was a composer and performer of many songs reflecting the singularity of Chile and its multicultural past. Tragically, although she is remembered beyond the borders of her native land for the composition and performance of the song "Gracias a la vida" (I Give Thanks to Life), she took her life in 1967. The American singer Joan Baez made that haunting song part of her repertoire in the 1960s, and it continues to be heard around the world. Parra's music reflected her own experiences and extolled the indigenous past of her country as well as the contributions of Spain. The instruments that she preferred—the guitar, the *charango*, and the *bombo*—and the meaningful simplicity of her music reflected this very well.

Santa María de Iquique

On December 21, 1907, near the northern city of Iquique, there was a violent clash between miners and troops sent against them by the owners of the mines. Many workers were massacred, and the incident would have probably remained unknown were it not for the fact that a native of Iquique, Luis Advis, composed a cantata titled "Santa María de Iquique," which was immortalized by El Conjunto Quilapayún (The Quilapayún Musical Group) in the late 1960s, a time when a growing interest in the nation's folklore began to focus the attention of many Chileans on all aspects of the country's history.

The music evokes the simple demands of workers for the basic necessities of life and the brutal suppression of their protests by an alliance of the bosses and the military. The tragedy is stressed by the cadence of the prologue, which evokes the beat of a funeral march, a harbinger of the events that will befall the workers. The eight performers of the Conjunto combine instruments of pre-Columbian and Spanish origin: two guitars, two *quenas*, a *charango*, and a *bombo*. Only two instruments of the standard orchestra are used: the cello and the bass. Luis Advis has confessed that his musical training had emphasized European classical composers and writers. As he matured, he began to turn his interests to native themes. *Santa María de Iquique* is the most resounding product.

Following the coup d'état in 1973, the cantata became difficult to find in retail shops in Chile; it was never clear whether this was due to government intervention in its sale or to a dearth of available copies. What is clear, however, is that after the return to democratic government, beginning in early 1990, the recording became available once again.

Víctor Jara

Another famous but tragic figure of Chilean folk music is Víctor Jara (1934–1973), composer and performer, like Parra, of many beautiful songs that have become a permanent part of the Chilean musical landscape. Some of his best-remembered compositions are "Te recuerdo, Amanda" (I Remember You, Amanda), "Luchín," "El cigarrito" (The Little Cigarette), "El derecho de vivir en paz" (The Right to Live in Peace), and "Plegaria a un labrador" (Prayer to a Farmworker), all of which have beautiful melodies and significant lyrics that reflect Jara's politicized art. In the days immediately following the coup d'état in 1973, Jara was interned in Santiago's National Stadium. It is said that his captors tortured him by breaking his fingers, a mocking symbol of their rejection of his political views and activities; soon afterward, he was killed. Roberto Bravo, a Chilean concert pianist who has also performed folk music, recorded a collection of piano pieces based on the music of folklorists such as Violeta Parra and Víctor Jara. The compact disc, titled *A mis amigos* (To My Friends), which appeared in the 1990s, is a great tribute to these two musicians who have left an indelible mark on Chile's musical landscape.

SYMPHONIC MUSIC

Domingo Santa Cruz (1899–1987), a key figure in Chilean classical music, was born in La Cruz, Quillota. Winner of the Premio Nacional de Arte (National Art Prize) in 1951, Santa Cruz was a key figure for more than forty years in the renovation of key institutions and in the establishment of new ones, all directed at strengthening the place of the musical arts in Chile.

His three string quarters, composed between 1931 and 1959, together with his other chamber works, have had an influential effect on the music not only of Chile but of Latin America as a whole. Equally significant are his four symphonies, composed between 1946 and 1968.

His music is intensely personal and sensitive, reflecting his life's experiences, especially the death of his first wife, Wanda Morla Lynch, in whose memory he composed his *Preludios Dramáticos* (Dramatic Preludes) in 1946, twenty years after her passing. Especially significant are the titles that he chose for these pieces: "Presentimientos" (Forebodings), "Desolación" (Desolation), and "Preludio Trágico" (Tragic Prelude).

Alfonso Letelier (b.1912) was born in Santiago. Like other prominent Chilean composers, he preferred to write for the female voice; his 1948 *Sonetos de la muerte* (Death Sonnets) are outstanding dramatic poems for female voice and orchestra. He is one of the few Chileans who has ventured into the composition of opera, and has also produced a major choral piece. Among his chamber works are a sonata (opus 19) for viola and piano, and variations (opus 22), one of the major works for piano composed in Chile.

The Symphonic Orchestra of the University of Chile

In 1920, Chile's artistic life was drastically changed through the creation of the Symphonic Orchestra of the University of Chile, with Armando Carvajal as its first director. Carvajal premiered in Chile many twentieth-century works of European, Latin American, and Chilean composers. The Symphony continues to be Chile's most important orchestral ensemble and, along with the Symphonic Chorus and the Chamber Chorus, is the backbone of Chilean musical life.

Claudio Arrau

Claudio Arrau (1903–1991) is indisputably Chile's most renowned classical pianist, internationally recognized as one of the world's best expositors of the piano concerti of Beethoven. At the age of ten, he left Chile for Berlin, where he studied with Martin Krause, who had been a student of Franz Liszt. When Arrau was sixteen, Krause died and the young student, not wanting to study under another teacher, set out to build his career alone. That year, Arrau won the Liszt Prize and, eight years later, the International Piano Competition in Geneva.

Arrau's repertoire was vast, including the works of Beethoven, Chopin, Schumann, and Liszt. In his long professional life, Arrau gave more than 5,000 concerts, establishing himself as one of the major keyboard figures in the world.

THEATER

Armando Moock

Armando Moock (1894–1942) is Chile's most successful playwright, achieving fame across Latin America and beyond, although the lack of interest demonstrated by domestic critics forced him to leave his country of birth and move to Buenos Aires in 1918. After the move, he returned to his native land for only short periods of time.

The Argentine capital proved to be a successful forum for his plays; with the help of the actress Camila Quiroga, he presented his works in Buenos Aires and established himself there quite successfully. His first work, *Crisis económica* (Economic Crisis), which premiered in 1914 in Santiago, was seen by only a few. His most important work, *Pueblecito* (Little Town), however, written in 1918, had almost 2,000 performances. The work presents a contrast between life in the country and life in the city; in spite of its slow-paced action, the public received it very warmly because it provided a faithful view of life in Chile's small towns.

Moock stated later in his career that 60, out his total production of some 400 theatrical works, had runs of more than 200 performances. This number has never been equaled by any other dramatist on the continent. Although his best work had been written by 1920, *La serpiente* (The Serpent), which he wrote in collaboration with Camila Quiroga, appeared that year and proved to be his most popular work, having had more than 2,500 performances in Latin America and in Spain. A movie made in Hollywood, starring Rudolph Valentino and Nita Naldi, bore a theme that was suspiciously similar to *La serpiente*. Movies have been made of this work in both Spanish and English since its premiere.

Moock was a master of psychological analysis. He depicts a society devoid of purpose, preoccupied only by its desire for the frivolous as an escape from ennui. Men appear weak and lacking in purpose; women, on the other hand, are strong-willed. *La serpiente* has been seen as autobiographical since Moock, like his male protagonist, never married, perhaps fearing that the commitment would destroy his artistic talent. In spite of his being one of Latin America's most outstanding dramatists, Moock was at first overlooked by the critics; years after his death, however, his work has been reexamined and his preeminent place in Latin American theater has been acknowledged.

Egon Wolff

Egon Wolff (b. 1926) wrote a novel, *El ocaso* (Twilight) at the age of seventeen, then gathered his essays and published them in 1945 under the title *Ariosto furioso* (Ariosto Insane), a play on the Italian classic *Orlando Furioso*, by Ludovico Ariosto (1474–1533). Finally, he dedicated himself to the theater, where he has achieved great distinction.

Wolff's first dramatic work, *Mansión de lechuzas* (Owls' Mansion), written in 1956 and produced the next year, received an honorable mention in the Universidad de Chile's Theater Competition. He was heartened by this first work's success and went on to write two more plays, *Discípulos del miedo* (Disciples of Fear) and *Parejas de trapo* (Rag Couples), the first in 1958 and the latter, a year later. *Parejas de trapo* was awarded first prize in the Universidad de Chile's annual theater competition. It was very well received by the public and the critics, and spurred him on to continue in the genre.

One of Wolff's best works is *Los invasores* (The Invaders), which premiered in 1962. The work depicts an industrialist named Meyer, who dreams that his home has been invaded by a group of the city's poor who, once inside, organize a socialist government. After narrating this nightmare to his family, Meyer sees a hand breaking a window of his house and a window latch being released; he suspects that his nightmare is becoming reality. The dramatist's intent, apparently, was to give notice to the bourgeoisie that it cannot remain indifferent to the squalid conditions of society's destitute.

José Donoso

José Donoso (see "Literature") has been identified as Chile's preeminent prose writer of the "boom" period; his career as a writer focused mainly on his early short stories (1954–1962) and his novels, from 1958 to his last work, published posthumously in 1997. In 1982, however, he wrote four novellas titled *Cuatro para Delfina* (Four for Delfina); one of these he turned into a play that met with great success.

Sueños de mala muerte (Dreams of a Bad Death) was the first of the novellas that Donoso wrote in homage to Delfina Guzmán, noted Chilean actress. The work was brought to the stage in December 1982 to rave reviews and was made into a movie, mostly available as a video due to its being only some sixty minutes long. Its title, *Historia de un roble solo* (Story of a Lonely Oak), has a double meaning, since both the play and the film version are the story of a man whose name is Robles, a real Spanish surname.

Donoso had often been identified—wrongly, according to him—as a writer intent on being a social critic, with the main purpose of chastising Chile's upper crust, to which he belonged. *Sueños de mala muerte* and *Historia de un roble solo* depict the dreams of a man whose sole intent in life is to improve his standing as a lower-middle class citizen by attaining recognition as a man of property, a status usually reserved to those who belong to the upper crust of Chile's society. The play/film is simultaneously comical and pathetic, for Robles attains his goal only temporarily, failing at the end of a long endeavor and losing more than he had begun with. Donoso succeeds, in a burlesque style, in identifying the falseness of this particular way of rising socially from the stagnant middle class.

7

Art and Architecture

BUENOS AIRES is often compared to Paris and the two cities share many qualities that would seem to support that comparison. It has a wide boulevard that is often compared to the Champs Élysées and fine theaters such as the Teatro Colón, and world-class shops along the famed Calle Florida. Its food is very continental as are many of its restaurants. Lima is a very colonial Spanish city, reflecting its creation by Francisco Pizarro in the first half of the sixteenth century. Facing the Plaza de Armas is the Cathedral that reportedly contains the skeleton of its founder. Another part of the capital city has the Museo del Oro (Gold Museum) which traces the city's fabled Incan past. At the Plaza Bolívar is the Court of the Inquisition, that traces the dark period between 1570 and 1820, during which heretics were tried and tortured for activities deemed criminal by that infamous court.

On a smaller scale than Buenos Aires, Santiago reflects its European past as well. It has a first-rate museum of fine arts and an attractive theater where the public can attend fine performances of classical music and ballet, with national and international artists. Smaller concert halls abound throughout the city where smaller audiences can enjoy music in more intimate surroundings, as well as theaters devoted to works produced by national artists.

There are regional museums, from its arid north to its cold and windy south, that capture the nation's history and national beauty. In Santiago, the National Cathedral and the Santa Lucía Hill fortress both date back to Santiago's early years under Spanish domination while, throughout the city skyscrapers evidence the capital's twenty-first century reality as well.

Like Lima, Santiago also evidences its Indian past. Pedestrians atop Santa

Lucía Hill, close to the downtown area, can reflect on the nation's past and present, as they gaze upon two imposing statues, one of Caupolicán, the country's most famous Araucanian warrior, the other of the conquistador, Pedro de Valdivia, the city's founder. The Chilean's psyche is ever aware of the inescapable duality of their nature.

MUSEUMS

Palacio de Bellas Artes

The standard-bearer of all of the nation's museums has to be the Palacio de Bellas Artes (Palace of Fine Arts), opened on September 18, 1910, as part of the celebration of Chile's centennial of independence. Designed by the French-Chilean architect Emilio Jécquier, the structure is located next to the Parque Forestal, a park on the northern bank of the Mapocho River.

Just inside the main entrance, there is a large hall with a glass ceiling, where visitors can admire works of sculpture before entering the many exhibition rooms that display paintings by both Chilean and foreign artists. The building has undergone both additions and renovations since its founding. Among the most significant are the building of a children's theater in 1938, and the rebuilding of the wooden cupula of the School of Fine Arts, which was destroyed by a fire in 1969.

Museo Regional Salesiano "Mayorino Borgatello"

Founded in Punta Arenas in 1893, under the auspices of Father Mayorino Borgatello, a member of the Salesian religious order, the Museo Regional Salesiano "Mayorino Borgatello" (Mayorino Borgatello Regional Museum) is devoted to the natural sciences, ethnography, and photography. When this museum was created, there was only one other in existence in the nation. Mayorino Borgatello was not a professional naturalist but an amateur who believed that the uniqueness of Chile's extreme south lent itself to the creation of a museum whose exhibits would feature the flora, fauna, and minerals of the area. Prominent among the holdings are flamingos, ñandúes (ostrich-like birds), sea lions, and migratory birds.

The museum is also dedicated to the ethnic groups in Chile before the arrival of the first Europeans, among them the Tehuelches, the Onas, the Kaweshkar, and the Yamanas, many of whom are slowly disappearing.

Museo Naval y Marítimo de Valparaíso

The Museo Naval y Marítimo de Valparaíso (Valparaíso Naval and Maritime Museum) is the creation of the German-Chilean architect Carlos von Moltke. It is located in Valparaíso, Chile's main port and second city. Work on it began in 1884, but due to a series of setbacks, many of them financial, the building was not completed for several years. In effect, the structure is an ongoing project, constantly changing to accomodate new additions and displays.

The exhibition rooms bear the names of Chile's many military and political figures, preeminent among them Bernardo O'Higgins, Lord Thomas Cochrane, Blanco Encalada, Diego Portales, and Arturo Prat. Displayed are paintings and artifacts from Chile's nineteenth-century wars, including what is considered the museum's most valuable work, the painting *The Sinking of the Esmeralda*, by Thomas Jacques Sommerscales (1842–1927). An artifact that is strongly tied to this painting is the *Esmeralda*'s clock, stopped at exactly 12:10.

PAINTING

José Gil de Castro (1785–1841), a painter from Lima, arrived in Santiago shortly before Chile's independence in 1818. He dedicated himself primarily to portrait painting, and a very representative example of his art is his oil-on-wood depiction of the nation's first president, *Bernardo O'Higgins* (1824). The patriot appears as a priest-like figure, reminding one of a colonial religious figure.

Raimundo Monvoisin (1790–1870) was a French painter, invited to Chile by Mariano Egaña, a political ally of Diego Portales, to found an Academy of Fine Arts. Although the academy did not come into existence at that time, Monvoisin did establish a workshop in which he gave lessons to many eager painters-to-be. Like Gil de Castro, Monvoisin devoted himself mainly to portraiture, though he also painted landscapes and works with mythological, religious, and historical themes. One of his primary works is the oil-on-leather *Portrait of Carmen Alcalde Velasco de Cazotte* (1843), a patrician lady whose portrait is a study in contrast between her pale skin, the darkness of her hair and dress, and the red of the background.

Preeminent among twentieth-century painters is Roberto Matta (1912–) who is one of the primary creators of abstract surrealism. He moved to Paris as an architect, working in the workshop of the architect Le Corbusier. Dur-

The northern façade of Chile's presidential palace, La Moneda. This side faces Constitution Square. Many other government buildings also face the square or are located within a few blocks of it.

ing World War II, Matta lived in the United States, as did many other European artists. One of his best-known paintings is *Birth of America*, painted during his last creative period, between 1950 and 1960. It offers a multiplicity of intergalactic beings surrounded by constantly changing green and yellow lights placed on a blue background.

ARCHITECTURE

Santiago, founded in 1541, has architecture that evidences its ancient past, its colonial period, and the skyline typical of any late twentieth-century/early twenty-first-century metropolis. Chileans appreciate their past even as they show pride in the country's present, born out of more than 450 years of existence.

An imposing building, covering a square block of the city's downtown, is La Moneda (The Mint), a magnificent and sober structure that dates to the late eighteenth century. Designed by the Italian architect Joaquín Toesca, it served at first as the national mint but, in 1848, was designated the official residence of the nation's presidents. The fortress-like building faces the capital's main thoroughfare, the Alameda Bernardo O'Higgins, on the south; a standing statue of President Arturo Alessandri faces south across the expanse

A *carabinero* (police officer), posing at the southern entrance to La Moneda. The ceremonial sword is an indication of his rank.

of the wide avenue. Across the Alameda is the Plaza de los Libertadores (Liberators' Square), which features two imposing memorials, one of them an equestrian statue of Bernardo O'Higgins, Chile's first president, who faces the Moneda. To the building's southwest stands an equestrian monument honoring Chile's other liberator, the Argentine general José de San Martín.

On the palace's northern side is the Plaza de la Constitución (Constitution Square), where every Sunday, Chile's *carabineros* (police) put on a spectacular display of disciplined marching. It is said that the force's tallest members are chosen for this honor duty, and this would seem to be true, since every marcher seems to be at least 1.80 meters in height (almost 6 feet). The square is adorned with statues commemorating some of Chile's most outstanding politicians, among them Diego de Portales and former President Eduardo Frei Montalva.

Facing Constitution Square on the west is the Hotel Carrera, for many years Santiago's premier luxury hotel. It still holds a five-star rating, and it is common for Santiago's "in" crowd to meet there for lunch or tea. Until fairly recently, the seventeen-story building was the nation's tallest, a reflection of the country's respect for its seismic location. Given the architectural advances that have been made in the last few decades, Santiago now has several skyscrapers of thirty and more stories. One vision that will not quickly fade from the memory of many of Santiago's residents and from international viewers of the news is the precision bombing of the Moneda Palace, which began on the morning of September 11, 1973. That day, the nation's armed forces, especially the air force, heavily damaged the building in their successful overthrow of the government of Salvador Allende. The building remained closed for a long time while it underwent a complete renovation. Chilean and foreign journalists provided the world with spectacular pictures, both still and motion, of the bombing from their vantage point atop the Carrera Hotel.

Only a few blocks north and east of the Moneda Palace is the Plaza de Armas (Main Square). (When Spain built its cities in the New World, it meticulously planned the center of each metropolis, beginning with a fortified square; thus the word *armas*, which means "arms" or "weapons.") Facing this main square are Santiago's Correo Central (main post office) and the Catedral (cathedral), the official seat of Chile's Roman Catholic Church. The sixteenth-century cathedral has survived more than one major earthquake and countless lesser tremors.

The square has carefully tended lawns and trees. Bands sometimes perform on weekends, and many of Santiago's citizens spend time in this green oasis in the middle of downtown. It has been a tradition, especially in years past, for families dressed in their Sunday best to have their portraits taken by one of the many photographers who make this square the center of their professional activities.

The Teatro Municipal (Municipal Theater) is some four blocks east and south of the Plaza de Armas. This strikingly beautiful white structure was built in 1847 and today is the home of the Orquesta Filarmónica (Philharmonic Orchestra) and the Ballet Municipal de Santiago (Santiago's Municipal Ballet). Between June and September, national and international musicians, opera companies, and orchestras perform regularly in its richly decorated hall.

Several blocks north of the Teatro Municipal is the imposing Palacio de Bellas Artes (Palace of Fine Arts). Dating from the nineteenth century, it is Chile's equivalent of the Prado and Louvre museums, housing much of the national treasury of paintings and sculpture. Traveling displays, such as the works of the Colombian sculptor/painter Fernando Botero, have been dis-

The Palacio de Bellas Artes in Santiago; the striking sculpture at the center bears an inscription that says, "United in Glory and Death."

played within the museum's ample halls and exhibition patio. (See "Museums.")

Almost directly south of Bellas Artes, and facing the Alameda Bernardo O'Higgins, is the Cerro Santa Lucía (St. Lucía Hill), called Huelén by the Araucanian Indians. This is the site of the founding of Santiago by Pedro de Valdivia, on February 12, 1541. The Spaniards built a fort atop the hill that stands only a few hundred feet above the busy streets of the capital. Today, the fortress is open to the public and forms part of a park where *santiaguinos* walk and lovers stroll during the day. At the foot of Santa Lucía, and adjacent to the Alameda, is Chile's Biblioteca Nacional (National Library), which dates from 1927.

Santiago's historic buildings are mostly in the center of the capital, all within a few blocks of one another. The city, which has more than 5 million inhabitants, 35 percent of the country's total, has expanded tremendously from its center to the south and, especially, to the east, to the very foot of the Andes. Originally most of the area east of the square known as the Plaza Baquedano (originally the Plaza Italia, and still referred to by this name by many) was principally residential, with some small businesses catering to the

This finely decorated building used to be a stately residence in one of Santiago's nicer neighborhoods. Today it houses a business establishment.

needs of those who lived there. With the eastward move of the city's population, many businesses, both large and small, have followed.

It has become difficult to separate business areas from residential ones, both north and south of Avenida Providencia (Providence Avenue), the continuation of the downtown Alameda Bernardo O'Higgins, which begins at Plaza Baquedano. Avenida Providencia changes names more than once before it reaches the city's outskirts and ceases to exist. Modern buildings, some twenty, thirty, or more stories, dot the landscape almost to the foot of the mountains. Such is the individuality of many of these glass and steel structures that the observer is literally dazzled by the architectural diversity. One skyscraper, in the area of Santiago known as Las Condes, is commonly referred to as the Chrysler Building, due to its similarity to the monumental building in New York City.

As the city's population has moved eastward, many homeowners have sold their houses to businesses. Some of the smaller residences have been turned into shops and boutiques, but still maintain the outward appearance of the original dwellings. The late nineteenth- and early twentieth-century mansions have become bank branches and other large business establishments. If some of the original homeowners were to return to their neighborhoods, they would still recognize them even as they were struck by the new signs over

The modern Congress Building, in the port city of Valparaíso; the original Congress Building in Santiago now houses the Ministry of Foreign Affairs.

their doorways and by the hustle and bustle of shoppers and clients entering their former residences.

During the late 1980s, as Chile was returning to democracy after almost seventeen years of military dictatorship under Augusto Pinochet, the government closed the original Congreso Nacional (National Congress) building and moved the seat of legislative power to Valparaíso, Chile's second city. The stately building in Santiago became the Chancellory, the nation's Office of Foreign Affairs.

The Congress is now housed in an imposing and massive, multistory modern building, with an entrance that features a dozen mostly white columns that support an open, geometric roof. The structure's contemporary style is in sharp contrast to the Moneda, the seat of Chile's executive power, and the old Congress building, now the Chancellory, perhaps pointing to Chile's vision for its future as a First World nation.

Housing

Chile is an extremely long country, with dry, almost rainless conditions in its northern third, moderate rain in the Central Valley, and wet, temperate forests in the south. Thus there are different types of housing.

Rain is not a problem in the north, so housing does not have to be built to withstand moisture to any great degree. The city of Arica, the northernmost in the country, receives less than an inch of precipitation per year. Flat roofs are thus quite common.

The Central Valley, where Santiago is located, receives an average of fourteen inches of precipitation a year, mostly from June through September. Private homes are often in the Mediterranean style, with tile roofs and stucco walls.

South of the capital, rainfall increases dramatically, reaching as much as 200 inches a year. Although homes can resemble those seen further north, and have the red-tile roofs that one sees there, it is not uncommon for thatch to be used to ward off the large amounts of rain. The area commonly referred to as the Lake Region, and especially the city of Valdivia, also has houses with the high-pitched roofs that are typical of Switzerland and Germany, reflecting the significant numbers of Chileans who immigrated from those nations.

All modern construction, whether residence, office, or store, one story or multistory skyscraper, has to meet the strict codes required for such structures to withstand the not-infrequent tremors that are part of Chile's reality as a nation located in an active seismic area. Buildings are not normally stick-built, as in the United States, but are rather reinforced-concrete structures that can withstand the enormous stresses placed on them by seismic activity.

ARPILLERAS

During the years of the Pinochet dictatorship, many Chileans who had been openly identified with the left during the three years of the Popular Unity government of Salvador Allende disappeared, the majority of them men. The mothers, daughters, and spouses of the "disappeared" felt they were voiceless in their calls for information concerning those loved ones who had most probably been killed by the armed forces and their supporters. Something similar happened across the Andes in Argentina as a result of the military dictatorship there, which was blamed for the disappearance of thousands in the late 1970s and early 1980s. The Mothers of the Plaza de Mayo demonstrated their frustration at the lack of information concerning their family members in that main square of Buenos Aires.

Chilean women turned not to the power of the word but, rather, to the power of art in order to voice their concerns and to make them visible to all of Chilean society. They took needles, thread, and scraps of cloth, and used popular art to tell their story to the world. They created visual images of their plight by means of *arpilleras* (literally, "burlap" or "sackcloth"). These *arpilleras* were crafted from materials collected by the women or donated to them by the Church, which supported them. What began as a simple demonstration of the women's love for their missing family members became a significant form of popular art. The *arpilleras* could be simply signs reading "¿Dónde Están?" (Where Are They?) Others turned to established symbols of Chilean folklore to present their message. One of these pictorial *arpilleras* is titled *La cueca sola* (The Cueca, Alone); it depicts a woman performing Chile's national dance alone, since her partner has been "disappeared." This *arpillera* has been brought to life by dancers who have re-created the scene by performing the *cueca* without a partner (an essential part of this folkloric dance form).

In the early 1980s, as the military dictatorship began to loosen its grip on Chilean society, a number of theatrical works were produced that included the *arpillerista* movement as an integral part of the performance. What had begun as a muted and simple way for women to express their voiceless suffering had become an integral part of Chilean folk art. A documentary showing the development and evolution of the *arpillerista* movement was produced by Films for the Humanities with a narration by the American actor Donald Sutherland.

A simple vehicle for Chile's women to bare their souls' deepest frustration before the violence and cruelty of repression has become an artistic medium, a significant contribution to the nation's folklore. Today, artisans continue to employ *arpilleras* to reach their public visually, much as earlier twentieth-century Mexican artists like Diego Rivera and Clemente Orozco painted their murals throughout Mexico in an effort to teach and expose people to Mexico's art and history.

Appendix: The Spanish of Chile

achaplinarse (**v.**).   To bail out of or pull or back out of an agreement or plan at the last minute. The expression comes from the name of silent-film star Charlie Chaplin.

agüita (**n.**).   Literally "little water," this is a hot herbal drink Chileans sometimes consume after a meal instead of drinking espresso.

ají (**n.**).   The South American word for "chili pepper," *ají* is commonly used in many foods that are typically Chilean, although the amounts are not necessarily large. The Mexican word "chili" is not recognized in Chile, except as an attempt to pronounce the name of the country. (A close approximation of the pronunciation of *ají* is *a-hee*.)

al tiro (**adv. phrase**).   Meaning "right away," this is recognized by other Spanish speakers as being a common Chilean expression; the closest literal translation is "like a shot."

amoroso (**adj.**).   A term that resembles the English "amorous" but really means sweet, or cute, or endearing, it is used in reference to a child or an adult whom one knows well, as in *Qué niño tan amoroso* (What a sweet child). It can even be employed for a thing, such as *Qué casa tan amorosa* (What a cute house).

animita (**n.**).   Literally "little spirit," this is a common sight along Chile's roads. The *animita* is a small shrine erected at the side of the road, especially on the site of a fatal accident. One positive benefit, especially where road conditions are particularly hazardous, is that drivers usually become more careful when they see the shrine.

ave **(n.).**   Literally meaning "poultry," *ave* is often used to mean "chicken" instead of *pollo*. One of the classic sandwiches, typically found on many restaurant menus, is the *ave palta*, which is composed of chicken salad and avocado.

bacán **(n.).**   *Bacán* refers to a person (especially a man) who is very self-conscious of his or her image, wearing expensive clothes and seeking to stand out in the crowd, to be cool. It can also mean someone who is very good at something.

bachicha **(n.).**   A derogatory term for those of Italian descent; *bachicha* has lost a great deal of its negativity because Chileans of Italian descent have been incorporated quite successfully into society for several generations. Two of Chile's well-known twentieth-century presidents, Arturo Alessandri (1920–1925, 1932–1938) and his son, Jorge Alessandri (1958–1964), were of Italian descent, and the two major pasta-producing companies of Chile, Luchetti and Carozzi, were established by Italians.

bencina **(n.).**   *Bencina* is the common word for gasoline in Chile.

boche **(n.).**   In Chile, *boche* is a "fight" or "melee," as in *Se armó un boche en la calle* (A real melee got started in the street).

boleto **(n.).**   Meaning "ticket" (as in "train ticket"), the word is also commonly used in the expression *dar boleto*, meaning "to pay attention," as in *Elena no me da boleto* ("Elena doesn't pay attention to me").

bomba **(n.).**   *Bomba* is a service station, although *estación de servicio* is also recognized.

caballo **(n.).**   The Spanish word for "horse," in Chile *caballo* is also used to mean something that's excellent or superb, as in *Te ves caballo* (You look smashing).

cachar **(v.).**   *Cachar* is probably an anglicism for "to catch on." A speaker typically asks, "¿Cachai?," a very fractured, and typically Chilean, verb form, to say "Get it?"

cálefont or ***cálifont*** **(n.).**   Chileans who heat their water with natural gas usually use this type of heater. It is commonly in the kitchen or bathroom, vented to the outside, and provides heated water as it is needed. Water pressure activates it, and the flow of water keeps it running until the faucet is turned off. Thus, there is no need to keep water constantly hot in a thirty- to fifty-gallon tank.

callampa **(n.).**   *Callampa* is a word of Quechuan (Incan) origin meaning "mushroom"; by extension, in Chile, *poblaciones callampas* means "slums," since they spring up "like mushrooms."

canuto (n.). *Canuto* originally meant "evangelist," referring to Americans who proselytized in Chile in the 1940s and 1950s; today, it means a Christian who isn't Roman Catholic, Lutheran or Anglican.

carabinero (n.). A *carabinero* is a police officer (see *paco*); *policía* is used less commonly.

chancho (n.). The common word for pork, pig, or swine, taken from the Quechua language, *chancho* is also used to refer to a waxer that polishes floors. The well-known fairy tale *The Three Little Pigs* is rendered in Chile as *Los tres chanchitos* rather than as *Los tres cerditos*; as it would be in other Spanish-speaking countries.

chao or chaíto (n.). From the Italian *ciao*, it's a way of greeting friends equivalent to the English "Hi," or "Hey," or "Howdy." *Chaíto* is even more informal.

choclo (n.). *Choclo*, meaning "corn" or an "ear of corn," is taken from the Quechua language; the Spanish words are *maíz* (corn), and *mazorca de maíz* (ear of corn).

chupalla (n. and interj.). Meaning a straw hat, *chupalla* is also used as an interjection, as in *¡Ay, chupalla!*, meaning "Oh!" or "Ow!"

cola de mono (n.). Literally "monkey's tail," it is an alcoholic drink made with brandy, milk, coffee, and sugar.

colorín/colorina (adj.). In Chile, these two words are more commonly used than the Spanish *pelirrojo(a)* for "redhead(ed)."

concho (n.). *Concho* is the small amount of liquid that remains in a bottle, the dregs.

confort (n.). A generic term for toilet paper, known as *papel confort*, this was originally a brand name that has come to represent the product and not the manufacturer. The word *confort*, by itself, is sometimes used with the same meaning as the English "comfort."

creerse la muerte (verbal expression). This means to think oneself God's gift to mankind, as in *Se cree la muerte* (He/she thinks he's/she's God's gift to mankind.) Saying that something is *la muerte* is to say that it's the greatest.

damasco (n.). *Damasco* is the common word for "apricot," although *albaricoque* is also recognized.

durazno (**n.**).   This is the Chilean word for "peach," although *melocotón* is also used, especially when referring to imported peach jam.

empleado/empleada (**n.**).   The masculine (ending with *o*) usually means "employee," while the feminine (ending with *a*) usually means "female servant" or "maid," although it can also mean "employee." The usual Spanish word for "maid," *criada*, is not commonly used in Chile.

en panne or *en pana* (**adj. expression**):   When one's car has broken down, it is common to say *Mi auto está en pana*, "My car's broken down."

estar para el gato (**v. expression**).   Often said as *estar pal gato*, this means "to feel puny or lousy," as in *Estoy pal gato* (I'm feeling lousy).

flaco/flaca (**adj.**).   Meaning "lean" or "thin" *flaco*, like *gordo*, does not have a negative connotation in Spanish. If one has a spouse, friend, or family member who is considered thin, addressing that person as *flaco* or *flaca* is a demonstration of affection.

fome (**adj.**).   *Fome* means "dull," in reference to a person, book, movie, etc. For example, *Ese libro es bastante fome* (That book is really dull) or *Mi profesor de historia es muy fome* (My history professor is very dull).

frutilla (**n.**).   This is the Chilean word for "strawberry," although *fresa* is widely recognized.

gallo (**n.**).   The Spanish word for "rooster," *gallo* is often used in Chile to mean "guy," as in *ese gallo* (that guy).

gordo/gorda (**adj.**).   The word for "fat" or "obese," is *gordo*; like other adjectives describing physical characteristics, it is often used in an affectionate way. For instance, if a husband says to his wife, "Hola, gorda, ¿cómo estás?" he's simply saying something along the lines of "Hi, honey, how are you?" However, it would be better to let a Chilean use the term first and avoid it until some familiarity has been established. Whatever the case, *gordo* doesn't carry the stigma of the English "fatso."

gringo (**n.**).   In Chile, the word is usually not employed in a derogatory way. It is used to refer especially to British and Americans but also, at times, to most northern Europeans or those who do not have a "Chilean" appearance. *Tiene cara de gringo* (He/she looks like a gringo) usually means the person referred to has either blond or red hair.

guagua (**n.**).   The common word for "baby," taken from the Quechua language, it is sometimes used in the diminutive form, *guagüita*. The Spanish word is *bebé*.

guanaco (n.). A *guanaco* is a member of the camel family, similar to the *llama*, the *alpaca*, and *vicuña*. All of these are known to spit as a defense mechanism; the guanaco, however, is the one most likely to spit when it feels threatened. Thus, Chileans also use the term to refer to vehicles that the police employ to control crowds of protesters by showering them with water from high-pressure hoses.

guata/guatón (n./adj.). These words of Mapuche origin mean (1) "stomach" or "belly" and (2) "fatty." *Guatón* is almost always a term of endearment.

guinda (n.). This is the Chilean word for "cherry," although *cereza* is widely recognized.

huevón/huevona (n.). Originally a vulgar term meaning something like "jerk" or "idiot," this has become so common that it is heard very often when friends talk to each other, with the sense of "hey, you," or "you know." It has about as much force as the English "darn" or "drat."

kuchen or cujen (n.). This word, from the German *kuchen*, refers to a fruit pie that shows the fruit through a lattice of strips of dough crisscrossing the top.

living (n.). A common English loanword in Chile and other nations of the Southern Cone, *living* is the most common word for "living room"; the Spanish word *sala* usually means "den," although some Chileans recognize it as a more formal term for "living room."

lolo/lola (n.). Used to refer to preteens or teens, the term includes all of the qualities that adults ascribe to adolescents. Those in their later teens also use it to refer to younger ones; it's not uncommon to hear a seventeen-year-old speak of a thirteen-year-old sibling as *lolo* or *lola*.

luca (n.). *Luca* is a thousand pesos (a bit more than $2), usually referring to the thousand-peso bill.

luquear (v.). A Spanglish (mixture of English and Spanish) word from the English verb "to look," it is used not as a replacement for the authentic Spanish word, *mirar*, but as an informal, "cute" variation among friends: *Voy a echar una luqueada* (I'm going to take a look); *luqueada* is a noun derivative.

maestro (n.). A *maestro* is a handyman, often a skilled worker such as an electrician or mason. In other contexts, it carries the connotation of a great musician.

mala pata (expression). Meaning "tough luck," this is a very common expression in Chile. After something particularly unfortunate has happened, it is common to hear a sympathetic friend say to the victim, *Mala pata.*

manjar (n.). *Manjar* is made by mixing milk and sugar and heating them for a long time. It's probably one of the first words learned by children since it has many uses, all of them attractive to a person's sweet tooth.

media naranja (expression). Literally "half an orange," the expression is often used in reference to one's spouse or significant other. *Mi media naranja* is akin to saying "my other half" or "my better half."

miéchica and mierda (n.). The first is a corruption of and euphemism for the vulgar term *mierda* (excrement), which in Chile has lost a considerable amount of impact as profanity. When Chileans euphorically say "Hurrah for Chile," for example, they add, for emphasis, *¡Viva Chile, mierda!* While the "profanity quotient" of *mierda* might be 5 on a scale of 1 to 10 (to be used in the company of friends), *miéchica* is no worse than "darn" or "shoot" in English.

miti-miti (expression). A corruption of *mitad y mitad* (half and half), this is used by many Chileans to indicate a willingness to share something equally, be it a piece of candy or the check at a restaurant.

negro (n.). Like *flaco, gordo,* and *gringo, negro* is a common expression of endearment. Since the word means "black," it usually refers to someone who is dark or olive-complexioned, or who has dark hair.

paco (n.). An informal word for police officer, the word carries about the same meaning as "cop" in English. The official word for "the police" is *la policía,* the words on police vehicles, but Chilean police are generally known as *carabineros,* a militarized force that during times of war has served as a branch of the armed forces.

pasarse (v.). This reflexive form of the Spanish verb *pasar* is commonly used to express appreciation for something done, as in *Te pasaste* (You outdid yourself). The use of the familiar pronoun *Te* indicates that the expression is normally used among friends or family members.

pollo (n.). This word means "young chicken" or chicken meat. It is also used in reference to a person who is young-looking, especially someone who is young but looks even younger.

pucha (interjection). Originally a euphemism with a vulgar origin, it now means something akin to "darn" or "drat," or even "man." It can be used by itself (*¡Pucha!*) or can be accompanied by a statement, as in *¡Pucha, que hace frío!* (Man, it's cold!).

queque (n.). This is an anglicism from "cake." In Chile, it is a pound cake or white cake, usually served at tea time with a light sprinkling of powdered sugar.

quiltro (n.). A *quiltro*, a word of Mapuche origin, is a dog of mixed origin. Chileans make fun of pets that are obviously not purebred by saying, for instance, *Mi perro es un Quilterrier* (My dog is a *Mutt*terrier).

rasca (adj.). This word has many potential usages. It can mean "tacky," as in *Qué ropa más rasca* (What tacky clothes), or "low class," as in *Es un hombre muy rasca* (He's a real low-class man).

regio (adj.). Like *súper*, *regio* connotes "special" or "attractive," and is used for persons. If one sees an attractive woman, it is common to hear *Qué regia es esa mujer* (That woman's gorgeous).

roto (n. or adj.). Literally meaning "broken" or "torn," *roto* is a term that carries both positive and negative connotations. A *roto* is a person from the lower class, visually identifiable by tattered clothing and, at times, a less than clean body, and lacking the social niceties expected of those who are at least middle class. At the same time, a *roto* can be a truly Chilean individual, the salt of the earth. *No seas roto* is sometimes a criticism uttered by one friend to another when the latter has done something considered unrefined or coarse. The term *Juan Verdejo* is often used for a person who typifies the *roto*.

rucio (adj.). This is the most common adjective to mean blond; the Spanish word *rubio* is used as well.

sí po or sí pu (expression). This is an abbreviated form of *sí, pues*, meaning "yes, of course." It is very common in Chile.

siútico (adj.). This means "pretentious" or "snobbish," as in *Pancho es muy siútico* (Pancho is very snobbish).

súper (adv.). Since the 1960s, this adverb has often been placed before almost any adverb or adjective as in *súper bueno* (super good) or *súper inteligente* (super intelligent), or *súper bien* (super well).

taco (n.). Not to be confused with the Mexican tortilla sandwich, a taco, in Chile, has two common and different meanings: the heel of a shoe or a traffic jam, such as in *Se armó un taco a las 5:00* (A traffic jam formed at 5 o'clock).

***tarro* (n.).** This is the everyday word for a tin can; the Spanish word *lata* is also recognized.

***trago* (n.).** Literally a "swallow" of a liquid, it is used in reference to a drink, as in *Vamos a tomar un trago* (Let's have a drink).

***tuto* (n.).** Usually a children's expression, it connotes sleep, as in *Juanito, es hora de hacer tuto,* (Johnny, it's time to go to sleep).

***upa* (interj.).** One of the first words acquired by young children, it means "Hold me" or especially, "Pick me up." The child says *¡Upa!* to a willing family member.

USA. This recognized acronym for the United States of America is pronounced as if it were the Spanish word *usa.*

***vermut* (n.).** *Vermut* is any movie or theater performance that begins between tea time and dinner, that is, at around seven o'clock in the evening.

***water* or *guáter* (n.).** This is the common way of saying "the john"; the second spelling is the Spanish approximation of the way the English word is pronounced (from "water closet").

***ya* (interj.).** This is used in the sense of "okay," to show agreement with something. "Okay" (sometimes written *okey* in Spanish) means about the same.

Bibliography

Adelstein, Miriam. *Studies on the Works of José Donoso*. Lewiston, NY: Edwin Mellen Press, 1990.

Alegría, Fernando. *Historia de la novela hispanoamericana*. Mexico City: Ediciones de Andrea, 1965.

Allende, Isabel. *Eva Luna*. Translated by Margaret Sayers Peden. New York: Alfred A. Knopf, 1988.

―――. *The House of the Spirits*. Translated by Magda Bogin. New York: Bantam Books, 1985.

Alone. *Historia personal de la literatura chilena*. Santiago: Zig-Zag, 1962.

Arriagada, Genaro. *Pinochet: The Politics of Power*. Boston: Unwin Hyman, 1988.

Barbier, Jacques A. *Reform and Politics in Bourbon Chile, 1755–1796*. Ottawa: University of Ottawa Press, 1980.

Barrios, Eduardo. *Obras completas*. Santiago: Zig-Zag, 1962.

Bello, Andrés. *The Odes of Bello, Olmedo and Heredia*. New York: G. P. Putnam's Sons, 1920.

Bitar, Sergio. *Chile: Experiment in Democracy*. Philadelphia: Institute for the Studies of Human Issues, 1986.

Blest Gana, Alberto. *Martín Rivas*. Santiago: Zig-Zag, 1956.

Bombal, María Luisa. *House of Mist* and *The Shrouded Woman*. Translated by the author. Austin: University of Texas Press, 1995.

Brennan, John, and Taboada, Alvaro. *How to Survive in the Chilean Jungle*. Santiago: Dolmen Ediciones, 1996.

Domínguez, Jorge. *Insurrection or Loyalty: The Breakdown of the Spanish American Empire*. Cambridge, MA: Harvard University Press, 1980.

Donoso, José. *The Boom in Spanish American Literature*. Translated by Gregory Kolovakos. New York: Columbia University Press, 1977.

————. *This Sunday.* Translated by Lorraine O'Grady Freeman. New York: Knopf, 1967.

Faundez, Julio. *Marxism and Democracy in Chile: 1932 to the Fall of Allende.* New Haven, CT: Yale University Press, 1988.

Garretón, Manuel Antonio. *The Chilean Political Process.* Translated by Sharon Kellum. Winchester, MA: Inwin Hyman, 1989.

Gazarian-Gautier, Marie-Lise. *Gabriela Mistral.* Chicago: Franciscan Herald Press, 1975.

Gómez-Gil, Orlando. *Historia crítica de la literatura hispanoamericana.* New York: Holt, Rinehart and Winston, 1968.

Guerra Cunningham, Lucía, ed. *Mujer y sociedad en América Latina.* Santiago de Chile: Editorial del Pacífico y Universidad de California, Irvine, 1980.

Huidobro, Vicente. *The Selected Poetry of Vicente Huidobro.* New York: New Directions, 1981.

Israel, Ricardo. *Politics and Ideology in Allende's Chile.* Tempe: Center for Latin American Studies, Arizona State University, 1989.

Korth, Eugene H., S.J. *Spanish Policy in Colonial Chile.* Stanford, CA: Stanford University Press, 1968.

Lévy, Isaac Jack, and Loveluck, Juan, eds. *Simposio Pablo Neruda.* Columbia, SC: University of South Carolina Press, 1974.

Lillo, Baldomero. *Sub terra.* Santiago: Nascimento, 1974.

Loveman, Brian. *Chile: The Legacy of Hispanic Capitalism.* New York: Oxford University Press, 1988.

McNees, Pat, ed. *Contemporary Latin American Short Stories.* New York: Fawcett Columbine, 1974.

Millar, Walterio. *Historia de Chile.* Santiago: Zig-Zag, n.d.

Mistral, Gabriela. *The Selected Poems of Gabriela Mistral.* Bloomington: Indiana University Press, 1957.

Monteon, Michael. *Chile in the Nitrate Era: The Evolution of Economic Dependence, 1880–1930.* Madison: University of Wisconsin Press, 1982.

Neruda, Pablo. *Confieso que he vivido* (I Confess That I Have Lived). New York: Farrar, Straus and Giroux, 1977.

Nunn, Frederick M. *The Military in Chilean History.* Albuquerque: University of New Mexico Press, 1976.

Pollack, Benny, and Rosenkranz, H. *Revolutionary Social Democracy: The Chilean Socialist Party.* London: Frances Printer, 1986.

Prado, Pedro. *Alsino.* Translated by Guillermo I. Castillo-Feliú. New York: Peter Lang, 1994.

Rojas, Manuel. *El vaso de leche y sus mejores cuentos.* Santiago: Nascimento, 1962.

Sigmund, Paul E. *The Overthrow of Allende and the Politics of Chile, 1964–1976.* Pittsburgh: University of Pittsburgh Press, 1977.

Smith, Brian H. *The Church and Politics in Chile.* Princeton, NJ: Princeton University Press, 1982.

Subercaseaux, Benjamín. *Chile o una loca geografía*. 1940. Santiago: Ediciones Ercilla, 1946.

Torres-Ríoseco, Arturo. *La gran literatura iberoamericana*. Buenos Aires: Emecé Editores, 1951.

Valenzuela, J. Samuel, and Valenzuela, Arturo, eds. *Military Rule in Chile*. Baltimore, MD: Johns Hopkins University Press, 1986.

Van Waerebeek-González, Ruth. *The Chilean Kitchen*. New York: Berkley Publishing Group, 1999.

Varona-Lacey, Gladys M. *Introducción a la literatura hispanoamericana*. Lincolnwood, IL: National Textbook Company, 1997.

Willems, Emilio. *Followers of the New Faith*. Nashville, TN: Vanderbilt University Press, 1967.

Zeitlin, Maurice. *The Civil Wars in Chile (Or the Bourgeois Revolutions That Never Were)*. Princeton, NJ: Princeton University Press, 1984.

Index

About the Author

GUILLERMO I. CASTILLO-FELIÚ is Professor of Spanish and Chair of the Department of Modern Languages at Winthrop University, Rock Hill, South Carolina. He has translated several significant works from the Spanish, including the anonymous novel *Xicoténcatl* (1999), Pedro Prado's novel *Alsino* (1994), and the short stories of Clementa Palma (1984, 1988).